B
Reference

R	4366806B
818	Turner-Penley, Floe
TUR	Ellen.
	Scrap cotton

R

WITHDRAWN

BALL GROUND PUBLIC LIBRARY
435 OLD CANTON ROAD
BALL GROUND, GA 30107

For Reference

Not to be taken from this room

SEQUOYAH REGIONAL LIBRARY
3 8749 0043 6680 6

SCRAP COTTON

SCRAP COTTON

Floe Ellen Turner-Penley

Copyright © 1991 by
Floe Ellen Turner-Penley
204 Midway Road
Marietta, Georgia 30064

ISBN: 0-932298-84-2

Manufactured in the United States of America by
TRI-STATE PRESS
Long Creek, South Carolina 29658

Acknowledgements

It is with great pleasure I acknowledge those who have inspired and motivated my writing of "Scrap Cotton." First of all, I began to write for my own children and grandchildren, merely recording the stories that should be known to better acquaint them with their heritage. Harry Conrad (my husband) and Tracy Hall (my young but very good friend) sampled my first couple of chapters. Conrad gave his whole hearted approval. Tracy was estatic, being a lover of nostalgia. She would not give me rest. I couldn't write fast enough for her. They both told me "make it into a book!" I did, Tracy, so, just as I promised, I dedicate it to you. And to Conrad, to Connie and Patricia (my daughters), to David, Rachel, and Harry (my grandchildren), to Kyle (my great-grandson), and to all posterity.

I especially want to thank my 'family' for their corroboration:
    Esther Blackwell Maddox of Griffin, GA
    Everett Turner of Marietta, GA (posthumous)
    Edith Bailey of Cumming, GA
    Elda Gaston of Griffin, GA

Sincere thanks and appreciation go to my niece, LaRue (Bailey) Hitt, for the artwork displayed on the jacket.

Scrap Cotton

Acknowledgements Continued

I would like to take this opportunity to thank my friends and acquaintances, whose brains I picked:

Ford Phillips	Leonard & Mildred Westray
Don Shadburn	Zelma Sexton
Eldo Grogan	Terrell & Edna Bell Bryant
Loy Grogan	I. L. & Flora Bell Wallace

Jerry & Wynell (Groover) Byers
Maggie Worley
Gladyce (Mrs. Dean) Barrett
Mark Sanders at the University of Georgia
The American Red Cross
and the "good ole" Georgia Library System.

Last, but by no means least:

Veleta Todd - who cheered herself hoarse helping me over the last hurdles.

Beth Davenport - who helped me put it all together and into the "marvel of the day", that good ole computer.

Thanks, folks, I couldn't have done it without you.

Table of Contents

1. Closing the Door 11
2. One Way Ticket 14
3. New Place, New Ground 17
4. My First Birthday 21
5. The New Truck 23
6. Good Things Keep Coming 26
7. Beauty and Abundance 28
8. Butterflies 31
9. A Good Time with Mama 33
10. Ole Ring 37
11. Plane Monstrous 39
12. Home Remedies 41
13. Lemonade 44
14. Playthings 45
15. Deer Me 49
16. Mad-Dogs 52
17. Things to Ponder 54
18. Rough All Over 57
19. Move Anticipated 59
20. Teacher's Pet Gone Bad 61
21. The Transition 64
22. A Christmas Not Too Merry 66
23. Moving Up 68
24. Digging In 71
25. Spring Cleaning 73
26. Road Watching 75
27. Making the Feathers Fly 76
28. Monday Washday 77
29. The White Mud-hole 80
30. Threshing Time 82
31. Hog Killing Time 84

Scrap Cotton

32. Reason to Hope 86
33. Noticing a Difference 89
34. Shopping Adventure 92
35. Indian Lore 94
36. Gold 96
37. A Sticky Business 98
38. The Dusty Miller 101
39. The Family Dwindles 103
40. The Funnies and Chocolate Cake 105
41. Christmas of '34 107
42. The Magic of Town 109
43. A New Car? 111
44. Canton Woman 113
45. Another Tragedy 115
46. Brass Tacks 117
47. A Lesson Well Learned 120
48. Steppng Out in Style 124
49. The Chicken Business 125
50. The Revivals 127
51. Dual Purpose 131
52. Real Cotton Mattresses 133
53. A Cowgirl? Maybe 134
54. Ole Kate, Ole Jim 136
55. Squirrel Dumplings 138
56. Here Comes the Bride 140
57. Growing Pains 142
58. Poetry in Motion 145
59. Lily White 149
60. Elmo Burned 151
61. A Growing Family Tree 153
62. The Open Door 155
63. The Summer Death Hoverred 157
64. The Opossum Hunt 160

Table of Contents

65. Surprise! Surprise! 164
66. Batchelor Ties the Knot 166
67. Let There Be Light 168
68. Convenience at Last 170
69. Music Appreciation 172
70. Political Clout 173
71. Busy Fingers 176
72. A 'Saxy' Issue 179
73. An Uneasy World 181
74. Then There Were Two 184
75. The Three Musketeers 187
76. Let the Good Times Roll 189
77. At War 193
78. A New Sister-in-Law 196
79. Harvest Time 198
80. A Woman's Work Is Never Done ... 201
81. Bus Station 204
82. Hello, Tomorrow 206

Foreword

Although there was great satisfaction in coaxing a living from the soil, the drudgery was overwhelming in light of its monetary reward. Being a highly motivated man, my father sought out other sources of income, but his requirements of us were unchanged, as were the rewards. Mama's butter and egg money, although she did her best, did not compensate for the material things we lacked. Therefore we siezed every opportunity to scrape together extra pennies in any way we honorably could. But to us all, finally came the day we could escape the deprivation we had experienced, each persuing our own direction in life.

It has been said that anyone could write a book, as long as one knew one's subject. I know my subject, being brought up in the foothills of north Georgia. I accumulated many poignant memories; these are vividly etched in my mind. It is now with delight I share them with anyone desiring to pull back the curtain to the past to get an insight as to how it really was with many who are still living today.

Chapter 1
Closing the Door
1942

When I sank down in the comfortable seat of the big Greyhound bus, I tried to act as nonchalant as possible, while I nestled my guitar beside me, the strap being still about my neck. The oversized shoe box containing most of my possessions, I had placed on the rack overhead. The door now closed, my stomach did something funny at the rush of the motor, and the surge of the bus as it pulled back onto and down the road.

A door was closing. Another great and wonderful door was opening. My heart pounded with anticipation, while at the same time, there was a tinge of.., not regret.., but - "pain of parting" as the strings of home were severed. Mama was left behind.

I observed that the scattering of people already aboard were quiet. They seemed caught up in their own thoughts. Although most of them, I was sure, were from farms the same as us, they took on this air as if they were city folks; and didn't speak everyone to everyone else. I sure didn't want to appear any different, so I shut them out of my mind, relishing the whir of the engine; and enjoying the luxury of the ride. I hardly noticed the familiar landscape racing by my window.

Elda, my sister, sat beside me. That quelled any fear or forboding I might have otherwise felt. Her big "poke" which contained her belongings, and a few of mine, had also been deposited overhead. While she too appeared relaxed and at

Scrap Cotton

ease, she did glance at me rather often, wondering (I'm sure) if I was experiencing to the fullest what was happening.

The excitement within me now quelled. I began to recall, as if to memorize, all the sights and sounds I had drunk in the evening before. The cows had been milked, that was my job. Elda had fed them; gathered her load of firewood; and gone into the house to help Mama with supper. Daddy was still feeding the mules and hogs. He would soon be by passing the woodpile, stopping at the porch where he would wash his face and hands, comb his hair, then go on in to await supper. So before I gathered my load of wood, I endeavored to record every sight and sound. This I would carry with me always.

It was picturesque. The sun was just setting, leaving a reddish hue on the few clouds gathered in the west. The chill of the frosty night ahead was already felt in the air. The mules were eating their corn Daddy had just given them; and were quite noisy about it. The woodpile being between the barn and the house, one could easily hear them at that distance gnawing and grinding away. The hogs grunted contentedly as they chomped their corn. A pig would squeal now and then because he was being rooted out of the trough. The chickens, some of them already full of the hog's dropped corn, were headed for the roost on the far side of the house. Others were clucking excitedly as they darted in among the hogs for more. The cow would moo softly at her calf as she ground away at her hay.

I looked intently about at the skyline, at the trees which already appeared still and sleepy. I looked at the barn, the crib, and the old garage

Closing the Door

that held an old blacksmith shop in back. That's where Daddy shoed the mules, sharpened plows, and bent and shaped any metal he needed. I looked at the old log "chicken-house" that we girls and Mama had built. I remembered all the mud we made and hauled to daub the cracks. I was reliving this.

I looked at the old log hen house on the other side of the barn. It was still covered in cow-itch-vine but the foilage and beautiful flowers were gone. The chickens did not roost there anymore, for Daddy said they'd get mites on the livestock. But Mama prevailed in that it was left standing, because of the beauty of the blooming vine. It made one beautiful flower pot in the summer.

The ducks had already waddled by to roost in Mama's rose garden in the back yard. I was listening to their subdued quack-quacking, which was more of a murmur, as if they were talking to each other confidentially.

Then came mother's call, "Supper, Floe Ellen"; a voice, an invitation that would never be surpassed in my memory. My attention drawn, I turned toward the house. It was cold enough for a fire; the rosy yellow flickering glow overcame the white light of the electric bulb. My heart warmed within me.

With Mama's call came the awareness of the fresh back-bone, and whatever else Mama would have on the table. I gathered my stove wood hurriedly, and went inside. The dusk now gathered, I wouldn't look back again.

Chapter 2
One Way Ticket

The bus stopped in Cumming. There were a few more people aboard now. Still few people had appeared to notice my guitar. I sorta wished they would; I was proud of it. It was the best that Sears & Roebuck offered. It didn't bother me much that I didn't have a case for it like Martha Carson. She was my idol, and I had been told I had something of her style. Maybe, just maybe, someday I might get on the radio too. I intended to make good at something, someday, somehow. Now, I was getting my chance.

The war was still taking a terrible toll, though there were reports that it was somehow beginning to be turned around. Churchhill, Stalin, and Roosevelt were agreed on the strategy - "Beat Germany first"; then all efforts would be turned to whipping the Japanese. British and American troops had landed in French North Africa. Americans were now fighting Germans, while at the same time American troops had landed in the invasion of Algiers. It was evident that the whole Italian army was cut off and would have to surrender, having been deserted by the Germans. Winston Churchhill was so sure of eventual victory, he had orderd all the bells of England to be rung. In the Western theater, the Americans along with Australian troops had easily taken the small island of Talage in the Solomons. The marines had gone ashore at Guadalcanal. Bitter fighting ensued, but the U.S. Marines held. Our losses were overwhelming, but the reports were that we only lost half as many men as the Japs.

One Way Ticket

We were on the counter offensive now, and were beginning to take back some of the islands that we had earlier lost.
America was flexing her patriotic muscles. This was some where in the back of my mind, "To do my part." Going to work in a cotton mill didn't seem too patriotic, but we all had to be clothed. And this was where my sister Esther and her husband worked. Their home was where we would be boarding. This, I'm sure, is what made it bearable for Mama to let her girls leave home to go to public works. Mama had been the one to broach the subject of our leaving home. She said it wasn't fair to us to stay home, and get by on so little when we could be making good money and getting a better chance at life. She said that she had raised us right, and felt that we could be trusted to do right. The burden to do right fell on our shoulders then and there.
The money we could make loomed big in our eyes. Esther was making twenty dollars a week now. Clarence, her husband, made about the same, but he added more by having a radio shop where he worked in his spare time. All in all, they were doing alright. They drove a good car and wore good clothes. This had pursuaded us of better things.
We had managed to get enough money to buy our tickets, (one way, of course), enough to pay Esther ten dollars each for two weeks board until we could draw. We had a couple of dollars for lunch money, and another ten dollars each to buy us a couple of dresses and shoes to work in. We were cutting it close, we knew that, but it would do. Then, the day before we left, Daddy came in and gave Mama two ten- dollar bills, telling her

Scrap Cotton

to give the money to us. She refused to take it, telling him to give it to us himself. He walked by and tossed it in a chair. We walked by it several times. Finally, Elda said, "We don't want it." I said, "I do," and picked it up.

When the bus had left Forsyth county, and pulled into Alpharetta, some people had gotten off, but more were getting on, including a few black people. I tried not to appear to notice as they quietly made their way to the back of the bus. I had seen very few black people in my life. I was well aware they didn't live or even come into Forsyth county; since they had all been run out in 1913, because of three black men who had reportedly raped and killed a white girl. I shuddered when I recalled Daddy's account of seeing two of them hanged. It seemed the other one had been lynched earlier by a mob.

I didn't know how I would or should react when I would begin to encounter them, but I had been told they were to be 'kept in their place'. My problem was, would I be able to know my place with them? It sounded to me like it would be awkward, how could I inflict upon another the hurt that had been inflicted upon me? Oh well, I would encounter a lot of new things where I was going. I would learn; I would adjust.

Chapter 3
New Place, New Ground
1926

Listening now to the drone of the engine, thrilling to the singing of the tires as the big bus rolled on to its Atlanta destination, I revelled in its comfort, and was not dissuaded from it despite the bouncing from the small bumps in the road. This was a far cry from my first recollection of my first move. I remembered the twisting and the bumping of the two horse wagon, and the fumes of the kerosene lantern that Mama and Daddy had set in the floor board in an effort to keep me and their feet warm. I was wrapped in a quilt. There was hardly room to struggle free, had I wanted to, for all sorts of household items were crowded about me.

The wagon wheels creaked and squalked laboriously as the mules picked their way up this last little hill toward our log house that we now owned and would live in for the next six years. I could never remember from where we had left, nor could I remember actually getting there. I do remember that we had left the big road, and were nearing the barn. (We would come to it before the house.) Mama exclaimed, "Look, Floe Ellen, our new home." I was not yet three years old, and naturally couldn't recount a lot of things that transpired along then, but I picked up enough later to know this had been a big turning point in our lives.

To buy this place, the family had worked, skimped, and saved what Daddy had made working at the Georgia Marble Co. at Marble Hill,

Scrap Cotton

until there had been enough to pay down on this house. There had been eighty acres of land, but probably no more than twenty acres in cultivation. The rest was in timber. Daddy had an eye on the timber. But there had to be enough cleared ground to make our food to eat, and then three or four acres for cotton (our cash crop). Daddy had plenty of help, six children at home plus him and Mama. Esther was already married, living in Alabama. Of course, R.W. and I were not big enough to be of any notable help, and Mama was sick a lot. Never-the- less, with everyone pitching in, he was confident that we were going to do alright.

Another thing I can remember is the smell of the apples once inside the warm house. (The older children had already built a fire.) Weeks earlier, they had come over and gathered all the winter apples and had stored them in the loft.

I think about the first thing that Daddy undertook at our new place was to order more fruit trees to put out. Mama's first project was to have Daddy buy planks and put in a partiion in the 'big room', making us girls a bedroom in the back. The boys slept in the little shed room off the front-porch. There was a shed kitchen on the back. It doesn't sound like much of a house being built of logs and all, but the logs were carefully hewn and fitted. Besides, we were proud of the nice tin roof. It was so very tranquilizing when it rained.

Well before it was spring, Daddy had mapped out the 'new ground' he wanted to clear. This was the grand-daddy of all jobs. First the trees were cut; the hardwood worked up into firewood; some of it was cut into stovewood. Then came the bon-

New Place, New Ground

fires as the brush was burned. This fascinated and intrigued us all. Everyone contributed, piling on and watching it burn. Then came the hard part. The stumps dug around and the roots cut. Then the crowbar and pryse poles were applied. Daddy coaxed and prodded the mules as they tightened and pulled the chains that were fastened to the stumps.

I can still remember the hurt sides the boys suffered from the plows that kicked back when they would strike a root while plowing. I remember, too, the constant cutting of roots and piling of them by us girls, even after the ground had been planted for two or three years.

Some time later, I was made aware of the fact that the family had once lived in south Georgia for a couple of years. Mama would talk wistfully about the vast flat lands they tilled down there. I couldn't help but wonder what had possessed Daddy to want to return to the red, rocky hills of north Georgia to farm. Cotton was our best cash crop, and we hardly had land smooth enough to grow cotton. None the less, Daddy inspired us to grub away, saying, "If we apply ourselves, we'll make a good living here." Everything took work, and everyone that was able to work, worked.

Just when it looked like we had enough hands to handle things, Egbert surprised us all by announcing he was getting married. (He was only seventeen years old.) Mama cried; but Daddy was furious, "Why! He hasn't even paid for his raising yet!" Egbert, knowing he wouldn't be able to work for Daddy, was fortunately able to get a job in the quaries at Marble Hill. In my mind, he was better off than we were, for they ate store bought food. To me that was special; and he

Scrap Cotton

seemed so very happy. I can remember watching and waiting for him to come walking by on the big road, always whistling. He didn't even own a mule to ride the six or so miles to work and back each day. It didn't seem to matter to him. He was now a man of his own.

Chapter 4
My First Birthday
1928

Being a leap-year baby, I had my first real birthday when I was four years old. Our birthdays usually were celebrated merely by Mama cooking us a cake. But I was the baby and due to the rarity of my birthday, everybody in my family made a big 'to-do' about it. Esther sent me my first birthday card with pictures and a nursery rhyme on it, along with a piece of material with a doll stamped on it. Mama promptly cut it out and stitched it. Then stuffed it with cornmeal bran that would be left in her sifter. I guess she had no cotton available. My doll was very pretty with rosy cheeks and golden ringlets like Mama fixed my hair. I loved it dearly, and I'm sure I was forturnate that the rats didn't get to it sooner than they did. It was three or four years later before I found her all chewed up. Needless to say, I was heart broken.

Daddy was still mad at Egbert, so Egbert would not come to the house. But he called me down to the road, and

Esther Blackwell

Scrap Cotton

gave me a piece of pink cloth with little white flowers on it. It was pretty enough to eat; and it made a very pretty dress. Daddy gave me material for a dress, also. Mama baked me a cake. Birthdays were great, but I would have to wait four years for another.

Chapter 5
The New Truck
1928

Something I could always say about my Daddy is that he kept his finger on the pulse of economics, since he was staying sober. In the past, he had been given to letting alcohol blot out his better judgement. His foresight in buying this place was proof positive that he had an eye for business now.

In the fall of '27 he started preparing for the sawmill he would have moving in. He took Everett, Edith, and Elda into the woods to start felling the trees and using the mules to snake the logs to the site, where they were piled dangerously high ready for the sawmill. Once the logs started being sawn into lumber, Mama would take R. W. and me with her to the sawmill. She would hand up the small planks and R. W. would stack them. There was nothing that I could do but play in the sawdust.

Everett, being quite a strappling of a boy by now, was busy hauling lumber by wagon to the railroad at Marble Hill. This was a slow process. Consequently, Daddy began talking of buying a truck. Mama was cautious, while Everett was excited and anxious, as were the rest of us.

By spring, Wilson Turner, Daddy's cousin who was a salesman for Roy P. Otwell Chevrolet in Cumming, was making visits to our house. (My! He looked like a preacher, in his blue serge suit, white shirt, dark tie, and suspenders. He even wore pretty bands around his shirt sleeves; we could see them when he pulled off his coat.)

Scrap Cotton

Something was cooking for sure. We kids tried to stay within ear-shot, but we knew not to get underfoot. Soon, here comes Mr. Turner, another man with him, driving our new truck. "Truck," did I say? Well, it was; but it had no cab or bed on it. It had just the hood, windshield, running boards, and running gear. It didn't take long though to have a bed and side standards put on and it was ready to go.

I heard Daddy discussing with Mama that the truck had cost $600. That was a lot of money, we all knew; even more than we paid for our place. Mama was scared that he had bit off too much; but Daddy assured her that the truck would eventually pay for itself and the farm as well.

Everett did all the hauling, but Daddy insisted on driving the truck to church or for pleasure. You can be sure we had people sitting all around the truck bed, and us little ones in the middle where ever we went. We really felt proud and drew a lot of attention when we drove up to church. Not many people at all had motorized transportation. Only a few other people, as I remember, drove cars to Corinth, (but their's were cars).

Although the truck was always much smoother riding than our wagon, we were especially proud now to see the chain-gang coming by working our roads. Still we were somewhat leery of them in their horizontal black and white striped suits. Some of them even wore a ball and chain. After all, they were criminals and perhaps dangerous; but they made the roads so smooth and pretty.

The truck gave us all a lift of spirits, but Daddy's outlook did a lot for us, too. He was

The New Truck

making money. I know he was, for he would bring home extra treats: salmon, cheese, peanut-butter, soda crackers, and Karo syrup (even though we had our own sorghum syrup). He even took Mama and Edith to the general store and bought them pretty hats. He bought Elda and me pretty beaded purses. He always bought R. W. and me candy or "chung-gum" as I called it. All of us were getting a lot of new things. The truck was paying off.

Chapter 6
Good Things Keep Coming
1929

We had a new president this year. Daddy wasn't exactly excited over it, saying Hoover was a republican, and that supposedly wasn't good. But we had our new truck, and that was good. But what was terrific was Egbert and LouAnna had a little boy. Now I had a nephew!

Just a few months earlier we had had a letter from Esther that she and Clarence had a big baby girl. I had been intrigued. But not getting to see her, it didn't make that big of an impact, (having a niece - being an aunt and all), but now I was walking on air. LouAnna was so sick, that Mama had to just about stay over there for several days. She wouldn't let me stay; and that was hard for me to understand. It seemed to me that there was a lot of secrecy going on.

Then there was this other thing going on that I couldn't quite understand, Egbert was having prayer meetings at his house. He would get down on his knees and pray, loud and long, just like a real preacher would pray in church. I heard people saying that he was called to preach. It didn't make sense. He had a tie, and he did have a couple of Sunday shirts, but they weren't white and starched like preacher's wore. It just didn't add up.

Then one Sunday at church, he got up and had a 'through'. He was crying; Mama was crying; even Daddy was crying. People were shouting. Then what always scared me half to death happened, Mama started shouting too.

Good Things Keep Coming

With everybody hugging each other, it was all just too much for me. I started crying. Some of the older ladies tried to tell me it was alright, but I wanted my Mama and she wouldn't pay me any attention. What if she just fell over dead? She shouldn't be exerting herself like that.

After so long a time, Mama did come back to me. Later she explained that Egbert was going to be a preacher. "What about his preacher's clothes?," I wondered. But probably with help from Daddy and Mama and maybe some other people too, he got some.

Esther, Clarence & Norma Ruth

I was proud of my preacher brother, my nephew, our truck, Mama and Edith's new hats, my and Elda's pretty beaded purses, and all of us in our new clothes. I had a lot to be happy for.

Chapter 7
Beauty and Abundance

Spring came at last, the sawmill moved out. All the timber in the immediate area had been cut and sold. The hard labor and pressures of the cold winter passed, everyone's spirits were lifted. The tension seemed to melt with the warming of the sun. Planting season always seemed to bring new life and hope to those who lived off the land.

Not all of my memories are of hardship, not by a country mile. I remember the roses that bloomed all over the place, the crocuses, the jonquils, crepe-myrtles, snowball bushes and many, many more flowers and shrubs. Some of these bloomers were already there, I'm sure, but Mama collected flowers everywhere she went. She, in turn, shared with others.

The dogwoods and all manners of wild flowers that grew in the nearby woods were glorious in the spring. The sweet shrubs and the honeysuckles gave out a fragrance that you never forget. As a matter of course came the butterflies in their flamboyant array, flitting from one flower to the other in their search of the sweet nectar. The apple, peach, and cherry trees were beautiful beyond description. The abundant blackberries gave their show of beauty as well. All these attracted the bees. Their buzzing from flower to flower gave promise of an abundance of honey later.

It was a joy, a delight to be surrounded by such beauty, and so serene to hear the barking of the squirrels, the chirping and singing of the birds as they made preparations for their young.

Beauty and Abundance

I can remember venturing to the edge of the woods above our house, just sitting there, listening to the sounds and drinking in the beauty with which I was surrounded. I had time for this, being still small and not yet burdened with a lot of chores. I would think in the spring that nothing could equal it, but each season brought its own rewards.

Come summer, many of the blooms we had enjoyed had given way to delicious fruits we relished. There were first the June apples, then the cherries, then the peaches, dew berries, blackberries, goose berries and grapes. There were the garden vegetables to enjoy as well. Fresh corn ('rosen nears' we called them), the beans, the peas, the shallots, fresh dug potatoes, cabbage, radishes, lettuce, and on and on. There was seemingly a non-ending list of goodies in the summer.

With the approach of fall, the list grew longer. The muscadines growing on the branch-banks ripened and the huckle berries. We had nuts by the bushel, had we desired: the chestnuts, the hickory nuts, the walnuts, the 'chicapens'. There were the apples that ripened in the fall: the black apples, the shockleys, and the yates. These were gathered and stored in the loft, where some heat could get to them, but not too much. Their aroma filled the house below. Mama kept them sorted; the bad ones thrown out, ones just showing a spot of decay were immediately brought down and eaten.

It seemed mother nature knew no limit. Through the summer and the fall we were kept busy gathering and preserving. After all, on the farm, that is what you are suppose to be, busy. Come winter though, (minus a sawmill or like oc-

Scrap Cotton

cupation), was the time to sit back and enjoy the fruits of our labors. Once the fruit jars are filled with fruits and vegetables... the churns filled with kraut, pickled beans or maybe blackberry jam, or perhaps muscadine preserves... once the barn is filled with feed for the livestock... the peas have been threshed from the hull... the crib is full of corn... once the jars are filled with honey, and the barrell filled with syrup... once the cotton is picked, baled and hauled to market along with any other cash crop... the general store paid off... then it is time to count your money and all of your blessings; including the wild game the menfolk brought in to eat: wild turkey, deer, quail, rabbit, and squirrels.

One might enjoy popcorn popped over the embers, or sweet potatoes roasted in the ashes. Perhaps you might enjoy a piece of ham broiled over the flames, or the cornbread Mama cooked in the old Dutch oven on a bed of coals along with a pot of beans hung over the fire. They might well be leather britches, (green beans broke and strung on a thread to dry in the summer). After being soaked all night, and boiled for half a day, these were mighty tasty. A glass of milk with another chunk of cornbread crumbled in it was enough to satisfy the palate of any country boy or girl.

Yep, winter, despite the foulness of its weather, would have to rank high as a good season. Maybe there was more to be desired, but, to my young mind, we had an abundance of it all.!

Chapter 8
Butterflies

My earliest experience of riding a mule was to sit astride one while he grazed on choice grass, and Daddy sat on the other mule close by. A little later, with me and the mule being more comfortable with each other, Daddy would let me ride the mule to the branch along side him or Everett to let them drink.

The branch to which we carried the mules to drink ran lazily across the big road where the branch had to be forded. Rocks were laid at the upper side for those on foot. The cars and wagons drove through. This was a charming little stream. There were hundreds of little minnows darting around in the deeper areas. Tadpoles inhabited the more stagnant holes. But the most interesting of all were the butterflies that hovered over and around the branch.

In my memory, this was the only place I ever saw butterflies congregate like this, or remember seeing this breed of butterfly. The largest of them couldn't have been larger than a half dollar, on down to the size of a nickle. They were yellow, black, brown, orange, white, while some were of many more variations.

They particularly took Elda's fancy. Elda hardly ever rode a mule, but she would walk down the trail, and on down the road to the branch. Once there, she would stand or squat for long periods of time, watching them. It was always a treat to me, as well. I looked forward to Daddy letting me go along to water the mules. I

Scrap Cotton

enjoyed the adventure as well as the enchanting little stream.

Chapter 9
A Good Time with Mama

The sawmill gone, and the crops laid by, Daddy found another way to make the truck pay-off. He and Everett began making trips to Habersham for apples and apple cider, or perhaps as far south as Fort Valley where he would buy a load of peaches, melons, or anything else he felt he could peddle around Tate and Marble Hill. Those who worked the quaries and other public works didn't farm, so they made good customers. And too, not many people had fruit trees, therefore, they would buy to eat or to can.

These trips sometime required that they be gone over night in order to find a full load. These were the nights that we were sure to have a great night with Mama. ("When the cat's away the mice will play" type of night.) The chores would come first. They were done hurriedly and cheerfully, while Mama prepared supper. We ate, chatted, and laughed - contrary to the solemn meals we ususally ate; Daddy thought it good table manners to eat quietly.

When the dishes were washed and the hogs slopped, the frolic began. Not a game of thimble, or pea porridge hot, mind you, but hide-n-go-seek, in and out of the house. Then best of all was Blind Man's Bluff. We would all but tear the house down. We would shove chairs, climb up on the funiture, and even run across the beds. Ordinarily, Mama would not permit this, not even to sit on them. It mussed the feather bed-ticks up. But on nights like this we pulled out all the stops.

Scrap Cotton

I think Mama had the best time of all, at least she sparked the good times for us. She would laugh 'til she would cry when the blind man would be closing in on one of us. But when the blind man would be closing in on her, she would look so breathless and desperate we would lose our breath laughing at her. Then one time when R. W. had her cornered and was closing in, she wet in the floor. Poor Mama! We never let her live it down. We laughed about it for years. Daddy would have said we were acting like a bunch of heathens. He would have called it all foolishness, but we called it a "good time with Mama".

Our energy being spent, we would settle down and listen to Mama tell stories of olden times. Stories she declared were true. She was born and raised further back in the more mountainous regions of Georgia, back before 'stock-law'; when cattle roamed free as well as the animals. She told tales of bears, wolves, and panthers. She told how this panther had pounced from a large overhanging limb and had killed and torn assunder the body of a woman riding her horse home one evening, devouring a portion of her body, and hiding the rest of it behind a fallen log. Her husband had been alerted when the horse came galloping home without her.

She told us of another woman riding a horse with her baby while carrying a load of sewing to a neighbors house who had a sewing machine. A wolf had gotten behind her, after getting scent of her baby. (She told of people having trouble with wolves when a new baby was born.) Upon seeing the wolf, the woman had whipped her horse into a gallop, but the wolf was gaining ground. Then

A Good Time with Mama

piece by piece she began dropping her sewing. The wolf would stop long enough to examine and tear each piece, then persue again. Then she began stripping herself, and then the baby. Yet it gained even to the horse's heels. Finally, out of desperation she dropped the baby. This took a lot of explaining, how that if she had not dropped the baby, the wolf would have gotten it anyway, as well as herself. Talk about your hair standing on end! We would draw as close to Mama as we could get.

She also told us of a little twelve year old boy, whose father was gone overnight. When the cows didn't come home from the mountains that night, it fell his lot to go seeking them. He asked his mother if he could take his father's muzzle-loading shotgun. She reluctantly agreed. He carried it, but without extra powder and packing.

After walking and calling, he finally heard the lead cow's bell ringing violently. He could tell that she was running hard. As they drew near, he stepped out of their trail to let them pass. They all came rushing by, except for one young heifer. The boy waited until the young heifer came into view. A panther was on her back with its jaws gripped about her neck. She was bleeding profusely. By the time the pair was near enough for the boy to distinguish all of this, the panther evidently saw him and jumped off, and hid himself behind the turf of an uprooted tree.

The boy, believing that the panther had chosen him over the heifer, made the decision to wait for the panther to rear his head. When it did so, the boy leveled his gun and shot. But, having no more ammunition, he ran for his life.

Scrap Cotton

When the father came home the next day, his son carried him back to the location. There, they found the panther dead, half his head being blown away.

She told us this one, too, about her own Daddy, our Grandpa Padgett, who was long dead before I was ever born. It seems he was on his way to sit up with a sick neighbor one cold, dark night. His light with which to walk was a pine torch (no flashlights back then); he didn't own a lantern. We would begin to draw close as she told how he began to hear a panther patting his tail in the dry leaves, like a cat getting ready to pounce on his prey; . . . how Grandpa's steps were quickened, but knowing not to run; . . . how the panther jumped across the narrow road one time, but did not attack; . . . how finally the panther let out a scream, after having stalked Grandpa to within a few hundred feet of his destination; . . . how he knew it was now or never. Grandpa broke into a sprint that probably would have set a new record, being careful not to drop his torch. He felt this was all that had kept the panther at bay for this long. There was a quickening of hope and excitement as she told how Grandpa had leaped a ten-rail fence that was around his neighbor's house, and made his final dash to safety.

There were many more stories of old, and Mama sure knew how to tell them. It beat the heck out of Daddy's nightly ritual of telling us how we would be fixed and out of debt someday. Never-the-less it was exciting when he and Everett would get home the next night with two money bags full of money, mostly silver, of course. But when he poured it out to count it, it looked like we must be rich already.

Chapter 10
Ole Ring

I was like all children in loving all the animals we ever owned. But my earliest and fondest recollections are of Ole Ring. He was a beautiful chow dog. A black man who lived in 'Smokey Hollow' at Tate gave him to Daddy while he was peddling apples. Daddy said Ring was mine, since he would be no good as a hunting dog. He had been a child's pet. We immediately took to each other.

I had always been a 'scaredy cat'. I wouldn't venture far from the house. But Ole Ring gave me new courgage. He and I would go 'hunting', I called it. Daddy had had the bushes cut back around the edge of the little field above our house. I would carry a stick, hit the brush piles saying, "Sic 'em Ring". He would plunge under the brush, rooting and crawling all under the heap. Then we would move on to the next pile, and repeat the procedure.

Ring was always obedient, as well as protective. He proved to be protective one day, when Mama had caught me climbing up on the well curbing, looking down into the well. I knew better, and Mama knew I knew better. So she broke herself a switch, took me by the hand, and began to apply it. Naturally, I started to yell (probably even before she hit me). Out of nowhere came Ole Ring! He grabbed the switch in his teeth, and held on until Mama let go. Boy, was I proud of my dog! But Mama wasn't letting me off that easily. She simply got another switch, and carried me inside, where she finished what she had started.

Scrap Cotton

But not to the approval of Ole Ring. He barked and jumped at the shutter on the window as long as I cried. Mama, from that time forward, first carried me inside to whip me, making sure the windows were closed. No wonder I loved that dog so much.

One day, we discovered Ole Ring was sick. Even I couldn't get him to eat. By the next day, he was down and wouldn't get up. He whined pitifully when we encouraged him to do so, or when he tried to move. He began to whine and cry at night. I'd cry when he cried, until sleep would overcome me. This went on for almost a week. At first, we feared rabies, but Daddy and Mama soon ruled that out. They were convinced somebody had fed him crushed glass in some food.

My mind could not concieve that anyone could be so cruel as to try and kill my dog. The morning I awoke and heard no whining, I rushed outside to check on him, and found him gone. Mama was right behind me. "He's dead, Floe Ellen. He couldn't get well. " I was crying uncontrollably, "How? Why? Where is he?"

Once I was quieted down, Mama explained how Floyd Anderson, our cousin, had brought his pistol and shot him while I was asleep. She talked as if he had done Ole Ring a favor by putting him out of his misery. Now I was angry. So angry in fact, I swore to myself that, when I was grown, I'd get myself a gun and kill Floyd Anderson. From that day on, in my mind, Floyd Anderson was a mean and evil man. He had carried Ole Ring away. I couldn't even put flowers on his grave. This was a mistake Daddy and Mama had made. I almost hated them for it. I loved and missed Ole Ring so much.

Chapter 11
Plane Monstrous

Living near Marble Hill, I had seen a train now and then, as long as I could remember. The marble quarries necessitated a railroad in order to ship the marble out. To me it was an awesome sight to see those big iron horses as they huffed and puffed under their burdensome loads. Yet, they warmed my heart in that it was a train that had brought Esther home to see us. This is my first memory of ever seeing her, since she had married and gone before I was two.

Airplanes, or "airplanks" as I called them, were scarce. But now and then, we would see one go over. This demanded all our attention: stopping whatever we were doing to stare at them as long as they were in sight. They didn't look all that big or awesome flying over at high altitudes. I always wanted to see one up close, never dreaming that I someday would. Truly, they were one of the wonders of the day.

Church was just over one Sunday when someone came galloping up on a horse, saying an airplane had crashed at Marble Hill. Daddy promptly announced that he was driving the truck down to see the crash site. As many as wanted to ride with us could go. Needless to say, the truck bed was full.

The single engine, two passenger plane had fallen over a creek, and was resting in the denseness of the trees that lined the creekbed. The tops of the trees were broken and split, but the plane was suspended on the branches. I guess the tree tops cushioned the fall, perhaps saving the lives

Scrap Cotton

of the two men. They were out walking around in their aviation caps, with their goggles pushed up. The wings of the plane were ragged, but not much other damage was apparent.

    I was completely astonished at the size of the plane. My former views of them led me to believe they weren't much bigger than the buzzards that often sailed overhead. Seeing this one up close, it seemed monstrous. Undoubtedly, being the cause of many nightmares that followed, always of a plane falling on me.

Chapter 12
Home Remedies

It was commonly known in the family that Mama was very sick after I was born. So sick that the doctor was forced to give her a medicine containing strychnine, therefore I could not nurse. I was raised on cow's milk out of a teaspoon. I don't know if baby bottles were available then or not, but I assume not. I never quite knew what all Mama suffered from, but she was in bad health for as long as I can remember. I do know that she had high blood pressure, and a kidney ailment. Evidently she suffered female problems as well. She stayed under the doctor's care most of the time. He, no doubt, gave her a diuretic along with other blood pressure medicine. Most likely, she was depleted of potassium, for she had these horrible cramps that drew and distorted her whole body. When this happened, she suffered agonizing pain.

We were so concerned for her; the rest of us were able to get along by using home remedies for the most part. There was Vicks salve for colds; tar poltices for bad chest congestion or possible pneumonia; a little kerosene on some sugar for the croup, or this combination along with turpentine rubbed on if we were choking with worms; then castor oil to make us pass them. We kept black draught and epson salts if we needed a purgative. We had Carter's little liver pills to work the bile off our livers.

Each spring it was custom for us children to take a round of calomel. One tiny pill every day for three days. We could expect to run behind the

Scrap Cotton

barn or smoke house until we were so weak we could hardly walk. Eating nothing but soup until our treatment was over. We sure passed the worms, pin worms and stomach worms, too, if we had them. Usually we did. Then we took a dose of castor oil to work the calomel out of our system so that we wouldn't 'salibate', whatever that is.

If we got a bad headache, we were put to bed. A brown paper bag soaked in vinegar and black pepper was placed on our forehead, then a bandage was applied over it and pinned tightly about our head. It burned like crazy, but it helped the headache. If we had a backache or sore muscles, we had Watkin's linament to rub on. If our back hurt down low, it was assumed it was our kidneys, so we took Doan's kidney pills. We had creodermic salve for all our sores, and we had lots of them in those days. It helped our risings too. But ususally we used a cornmeal poltice to draw them to a head so we could squeeze out the core. There was soda for our burns, and kerosene for deep cuts and puncture wounds. If we got in nettleweed or was stung by a pack- saddle, stinging worm, or some sort of bee, Mama would apply a plaster of snuff to it. Camphor was good for these things too.

Camphor was good for many things, as a matter of fact. We were never without it. It was used like a smelling salt if one felt faint. We used it on Mama when she would have her cramping spells. It was our most effective medicine for our monthly spells, rubbing it on us. Camphor was also a predictor of weather change: cloudy or clearing in the bottle. (It is homemade by shaving off slivers of camphor gum, then finish filling the bottle with whiskey.)

Home Remedies

Whiskey was used in many ways as medicine in our house. A sweetened toddy was beneficial for monthly cramps. We used it in a brew of ginger and liver powder that would almost certainly break up a case of the flu. We would drink it, then jump in bed and cover our heads, going to sleep to awake a few hours later drenched in sweat. We stayed under the covers though. Next morning we were well, maybe a little drained.

Mama knew a lot about herbs, but I never learned about them myself, even though I usually went with her to gather them. She mostly used them on herself. Maybe she didn't trust what she knew about them enough to use them to doctor us.

Another preventative we learned about was poke-"sallet." Edith was very sick one spring. She had no appetite and was losing weight. When she failed to respond to our home remedies, Daddy carried her to see a Dr. McClain in Marble Hill. She was diagnosed as having typhoid fever, a very present and dreaded disease. He began treatment immediately. She lost a lot of her hair, and it was months before she was well. He told Daddy if we would eat three messes of poke-"sallet" every spring, he would doctor us free if we got typhoid. You better believe we ate it, like it or not. And I didn't!

Chapter 13

Lemonade

Come the Fourth of July this year, Daddy said we were going to celebrate. The crops were laid by, and things were looking up for us. The sawmill would be moving back in that fall to a new location. More hard work loomed ahead, but right now we had a 'breather', so we were going to celebrate.

Daddy bought some lemons, the first ones I had ever seen. He bought a loaf of bread and peanut butter. Mama made some teacakes; she and the older girls made sandwiches. Then they got together our white table cloth, our best glasses and packed them into a box, just like we were going to meeting where they were having dinner on the ground. Then we were off to our biggest and best spring, almost a mile away.

When those lemons were squeezed into the jug of cold, cold spring water, the aroma was the most tantalizing I had ever smelled. The sugar being stirred in and dissolved, we got to sit back and enjoy. Edith, who still wasn't eating very well, was able to enjoy the lemonade. That made us all happy. (We had really been concerned, her being sick for so long.) Maybe the older ones in the family missed the ice that is usually associated with lemonade, but I didn't. I could never remember seeing ice; but the rest of the family had been able to enjoy a nickle's worth every now and then when we lived at Marble Hill.

Chapter 14

Playthings

Weekends around our old log house were usually sweet to recall. The weather permitting, there was this weekend ritual. The yards were swept clean; the floors scrubbed white; and fresh doilies put atop the furniture. Then, with everything clean, came the Saturday night baths. Come Sunday, Mama always cooked up something special: maybe chicken and dumplins, or a chicken pie. She would make a cake or butter rolls or maybe fried pies. We had church one Sunday a month at Corinth. On these Sundays we went to church. Otherwise, we visited our neighbors, or our neighbors came calling on us. In either case, we 'younguns' got together to play baseball (our ball was merely a ball made of string), marbles, anty-over, horseshoes, or to ride truck wagons. Sometimes we would just go to a sawdust pile where we rolled, slid, or dug tunnels. There was no shortage of things to do; no matter what age you were.

We smaller children played in our playhouses, which we treated in the same manner as if they were our homes. They were neatly outlined with rocks or boards, having two or three rooms. Our furniture was made of anything that we could find: scraps of lumber, buckets, or whiskey cans. These usually were used for our stoves. Our pots and pans were nickle snuff boxes and their lids.

In the springtime Mama showed me how to pick budding oak leaves and press them firmly in the corners of the doilies that she would make from worn out sheets. When you removed the

Scrap Cotton

leaf, there was a stained imprint. Now I had doilies just like Mama. Scraps of broken dishes were set on the table where we pretended to eat. We would use the larger ten cent snuff cans as our churns and pitchers. The pretty little blue Vicks salve jars were used as vases for small delicate flowers, which we found and picked. There was a use made for everything we could salvage.

As we got older, we didn't pretend that much. We actually built fires in our buckets, which we would cut holes in for doors and smoke stacks, and use as a stove. Then we would gather vegetables from the garden, half cook them, then eat them (no salt or seasoning of any sort). Its a wonder we didn't get ptomaine poisoning or something, considering the pots and pans we used.

We found that bucket lids made great steering wheels for our imaginary cars. We had no trouble buzzing like a car, and squealing our brakes until we would run out of breath. Bucket lids were great, too, to nail on the side of a strip. The lid was the wheel; the nail was the axel. The strip now could be a wheelbarrow, or better still a car. The old wheelbarrow itself could be used, with Daddy's permission. You could push it empty or haul a passenger. This though could be a little dangerous, being easy to tilt over when you cut a curve too tight.

Most of the young men and/or larger boys in our community built and had their own truck wagons. These were akin to the better know soapbox racer but being more crude. It had as its wheels about an inch and a half thick cut from a sizeable hardwood tree. A hole was put in the middle with an auger, for the axel to fit into. The

Playthings

axel was sawn from a hickory sappling, then carefully hewn to fit the hole. A nail or cotter-key kept the wheel in place. The bed or body of the wagon was a plank tapered at the front end, with a bolt fastening it to the front axel. A bar was nailed across the middle to hold onto. The square end was secured by nails to the back axel. You found yourself a hill, held on with your hands, guided with your feet, then you were in for a bumpy ride. Some of the boys improved on this by equipping it with a steering wheel, brakes, and scrap tire rubber wrapped around the wheels.

On Sunday evenings, the young people would gather where ever was the best truck wagon road, but the small kids could only watch at these gatherings. There were always trees for the rest of us to climb. We would find a nice tall hickory sappling. We had our favorites. The big boys would ride them out a few times to limber them up. Then the top would be tied down, a board nailed across it as a seat or a scotch, then one would get on, head downward. Next, the rope was released, and "Whoopeee!," what a ride. The tree whipping back and forth. Dangerous? Yes, but a lot of fun.

There were tops whittled from a half of a wooden spool on which thread had come. You inserted a stem through it, tapered it off, and you had yourself a top. Pea shooters could be made with canes from the cane break. These canes made great fishing poles, as well. The boys made flips from a simple strip of rubber cut from an old worn-out innertube. The pocket was made from the tongue of an old shoe. Or by using two strips of rubber, and a fork cut from a hickory limb, they could make a double barrel sling shot.

Scrap Cotton

Then there was the simple curved stick from a hardwood limb, whittled and smoothed on the outside, then used to push an old tire rim. R.W. and I used to wear out a lot of sticks while wearing our old rims slick as buttons. The tires themselves were great for rolling, or better still, for curling up inside while someone pushed you. Or, of course, they made great swings.

Daddy smoked Prince Albert, and like everything else, we saved the cans. Mama used them to store seeds; we used them for dominoes. Lining them up then tilting them, causing each can to tilt against another. We girls had our corncob or shuck dolls, rag dolls, and maybe a store bought doll.

We had a lot of things to play with, and found numerous ways to entertain ourselves, even if one had to play alone. I don't ever remember hearing the word boredom; and I sure didn't know what it was before I became a teenager. By the time our chores were done, we had no problem wondering, "What can we do?"

Chapter 15

Deer Me

The hills in which we lived harbored a wide range of wildlife. Some were quite dangerous, while others posed no threat to human life. The animals that were most visible were the deer that ran free, sometimes devouring much of the crops that were grown.

As I understood it, Sam Tate had constructed a reserve for the deer in an attempt to protect them. There were many corralled in a fence about ten feet high. He employed Scott Buice to live there and oversee the deer. It was against the law to kill even the deer that ran free, but people killed and ate them anyway.

There was this big buck that a lot of people tried to bring down. He had so many points on his antlers, it was said that it looked like he carried a large bush on his head. His antlers would have made quite a trophy, but it was more for safety's sake that he became a target for so many guns. He would attack dogs, killing several. He chased more than one hunter up a tree. We even feared him when we were out working in the fields.

One day Everett was out rabbit hunting, when this notorious buck came up on him. Everett stopped dead still, holding his single barrel shot gun ready to shoot as soon as the buck came within range. It was evident the buck had a bead on Everett as well. He would advance, stop, snort, and paw the earth, then advance again. Everett admitted he was shaking with fright, but he had no place to run, being in an almost open sage brush field. Finally, when he was sure the buck

Scrap Cotton

was in range, he leveled his gun and pulled the trigger. It snapped, again he pulled the trigger, it snapped again. He felt he didn't have time to take the shell out and turn it, so he did the next best thing. He dropped the gun and ran for a nearby small field pine sapling. He climbed it as far as he safely could without breaking the tree. There he hung on for dear life, while the buck smashed at its trunk, pawed dirt and snorted. Finally, the buck gave up and walked proudly away. Everett reclaimed his gun and came quickly home.

A more docile and bewitching encounter with the local wildlife occurred one morning when we awoke and started about our chores. We saw a small herd of deer in the field directly in front of our house. It was nothing unusual to see deer milling around in the fields, or near our house, but this morning they were so very close. There were some baby deer along; I remember they were all spotted. A more beautiful sight I've never seen. Edith had her milk bucket ready to go milk. We all tried to remain as motionless as we could, while Edith moved slowly in the direction of the terrace around our front yard. She held her bucket down, and a little doe came timidly up to her, and smelled in her bucket. It was a thrill we would long remember.

Though these encounters were sometimes frightening, they somehow made you feel closer to God, living so closely with nature. Except for the 'big buck' that everyone feared, the deer seemed the most precious of wildlife. True, they were a nuisance, munching off your crops. But this was all out-weighed by the rattle snakes reportedly found chopped up by the sharp hooves

Deer Me

of the deer. One could not help but feel a fondness for this beautiful and graceful creature.

Chapter 16
Mad-Dogs

'Mad-dog' was a common expression. Every now and then there would be word of mouth, alerting us that a mad-dog was on the run. People watched their animals and livestock closely upon such reports, killing them at the first sign of strange behavior.

This fall the word was out that a large and ferocious dog was on the run. Men mounted their mules armed with their shotgun, endeavoring to track the dog down. Several dogs entangled him. Many chickens were killed, and one man's cow was bitten, which later went mad. The settlement was frozen in terror.

Mama had always held that a mad-dog couldn't run more than a few days. But there were reported sightings of this dog for about a month. So long, in fact, that other dogs were already going mad, but reportedly they were soon shot.

It was fall of the year and crops had to be gathered, so look-outs were posted in the fields, while others worked. I was our only lookout while Mama and the other children picked cotton in our patch bordering the big road. I was stationed on the cotton sheet in the middle of where they were picking. It was all planned. I was to scream, "Mad-dog!" Mama would rush to me, while the other children scooted to the house. She assured me that she could handle him, even though he was a large dog. She'd "love him to death," she declared. Explaining she would squeeze his neck until he was dead. It was horrible to visualize

Mad-Dogs

what would happen if he did come. Thank God, it never happened.

It was not this same dog, but a very small dog that bit Terrell Bryant. It came up to him, and he reached down to pet it. He was bitten before he noticed the foam coming out of its mouth. Too late! Fortunately, rabies treatment was available. His doctor obtained the vaccine and gave him a total of twenty-one shots, deep in his stomach. Other than that he suffered no ill effects, but I can tell you, I was afraid of him for a long time. Afraid that he might go mad, too, and bite me. Terrell made a big joke of it, pretending he was going to bite his more adult friends.

One of the stories that Mama used to tell us, was of this young man that got rabies and died from it. She told of how he couldn't drink or go around water without going into convulsions. It was one story that I wish she had never told me. I have always had a horror of rabies, refusing to let a dog or cat even put their nose on me if I can help it. Rabies is such a terrible thing to have happen to anybody or anything.

Chapter 17
Things to Ponder
1929-1930

The mailbox was always a thing of intrigue to us. It was our primary link with the outside world. We could expect a postcard from Esther every week or so, and an occasional letter bearing a two cent stamp. The market bulletin and a weekly paper, that was enough to cause us to walk the mile to our box every mail day.

The news in the paper was drawing a lot of attention from Mama and Daddy. There were words foreign to me like 'stock market' and 'depression'. The only stock I knew about was our livestock. Depression, Mama explained, meant people could be going hungry. So! We already knew some people that didn't have a lot to eat.

Times were already so bad for lots of people that some of them couldn't afford a mule. They plowed with oxen, and rode in ox carts. Daddy's added interests, outside of farming, kept us afloat pretty good. Though Daddy would say we might have to "tighten our belts", whatever that meant.

The biggest thing with me was I had got to start to school that fall. I was learning to read my 'Baby Ray' primer. I was getting to eat out of the lunch bucket with my brothers and sisters. (Syrup and butter biscuits never tasted this good at home.) Mama would pack us fatback biscuits, and sometimes ham. It was all good.

Another thing I had was the prettiest, best smelling teacher in the world. She dressed pretty every day; and ate loaf bread sandwiches. She must have been rich! Mama said that all

Things to Ponder

teachers must go to college first. Besides this, they were from the city. I guess that explained it.

My teacher, Miss Bess, and the big folks teacher, Miss Tina Pat Lindsey, boarded with Coleman Bryant. I figured Coleman Bryant had to be rich, too. He owned this radio everyone was talking about, saying you could hear people talking from another state. This I couldn't believe, until one night Daddy drove us over there to hear it. There was a string band playing, and people singing. While the old folks were discussing it, I decided I'd find out for myself. "These folks weren't in another state; they were little men inside this box trying to fool us; and I'd prove it!!" Timid as I was, I still eased around in back, but I proved nothing. This was a mystery, that's what it was.

The Bryant's really impressed me. Terrel, their big boy, had this pretty red-plaid lumber jacket he wore to school. It was prettier than the other boys jackets, I thought. Then one Sunday, he showed up at church wearing a new jacket with, of all things, a zipper on it! All the big folks were gathered around him, pulling it up and down. I wanted to real bad, but I was too shy.

I thought I had seen everything when Everett bought a 'Kodak'. When he had his first film developed, he had a picture of him and Miss Loiuse Hopkins, she was my teacher now. I think he was sweet on her. He was about grown, and still hadn't completed the eighth grade. Not that he was dumb or anything, it was just that the older children didn't get to go to school a lot. They had to stay home so much to work.

Everett still managed to come home with another marvel, a graphophone. What it did

Scrap Cotton

amazed me! He'd wind it up, and would play records that just made you want to dance. Everett would shuffle his feet to the music and Mama would scold. (They didn't allow dancing at all.) Yes, I had seen a lot of mysterious things in my young life.

Everett & Louise Hopkins

Chapter 18
Rough All Over
1931

By late 1931, things were getting rough all over. The name Hoover was making an imprint on my mind. We were beginning to 'tighten our belts'. Work was short; cotton was down. We had plenty to eat because we grew it, but money was in short supply. Daddy's peddling was 'off', for people just weren't able to buy as before. Daddy took it to heart, and said it was a conspiracy. He had money owing him, and couldn't collect it. He was beginning to hit the bottle; and Mama was worried sick.

Then came a glimmer of hope. Sam Tate wanted to buy us out. Our eighty acres had about doubled in size, with two more houses and two tenants. Daddy was asking twenty-seven hundred and was pretty sure he could get it. We kids would stop picking cotton and peas and just sit on our pick-sacks talking, trying to comprehend how much twenty-seven hundred dollars would be. It was a lot of money, we knew that. But soon the sales talk died down.

Prohibition was in, but there was a lot of talk about boot legging, whiskey makers and haulers. We knew of some that were making it big in Dawson county, but we never knew of any in our own community. We heard, too, about the real big-time gangsters. There were gang wars, and a lot of lawmen were killed in their confrontation with them.

It was about now that Esther and Clarence were being starved out in Alabama, making their

Scrap Cotton

move to Griffin. Clarence had found work in a cotton mill there. A lot of people were out of work now, hungry and desperate.

At school, it was obvious some people were hungry. We sometimes shared our lunch bucket with some less fortunate children. I still recall these three boys who came. When the teacher was teaching Health, she inquired of each child had they had cereal for breakfast. The least one of the three said, "We had grease and syrup. Is that cereal?" His older brother spoke up and said, "Awh, ——. We had gravy too!" I guess there were a lot of people eating grease and syrup with cornbread for breakfast. Grease was not all that plentiful, but syrup was; and corn was cheap. If you were any kind of a farmer at all, you could have these things.

Yes, we had plenty to eat; but Daddy still owed some money. Now he was obsessed with getting out of debt. I guess Sam Tate knew he could get our place for less, so he was just waiting while Daddy stewed.

Chapter 19
Move Anticipated
1932

By now a lot of people had lost, or were losing their farms. Banks were foreclosing on them. Some could be picked up for back taxes. Daddy kept talking about us getting another place. He kept looking around a lot. He felt he was frozen-out around here, and that he could do better elsewhere. The thoughts of a nicer and bigger place excited me. But, consequently, I would be leaving behind all my friends, and the only home I had ever known. This tore at me.

The summer wore on, and was routine for the most part. By now Daddy's young fruit trees were bearing. There was fruit everywhere, it seemed. Mama's, and we girls', time was taken up, harvesting, peeling, and canning. Mama made lots of jellies and jams, filling every jar and churn she had. The green beans were pickled, or strung up to dry for leather britches. (For some reason, Mama didn't ever can green beans.)

By the time protracted meetings came in August, the corn fodder was all ready to be pulled. There would be close to two thousand bundles. (A hot job to say the least!) The fodder sawing and cutting at you with the pack-saddle stings made it a dreaded job. With the revival running morning and night, and the fodder pulling before and between services, there was time for little else. People managed and they went. The place would be covered by mules and wagons, and by now a sprinkling of cars. The altar would be filled with mourners weeping their way

Scrap Cotton

through to God. There were no 'repeat-after-me' conversions, or short cuts to be saved. You got saved the hard way; then you knew it when you did! There was great rejoicing, and it would make me feel happy, too. (As long as Mama didn't cry and shout; this always worried me.)

Come fall, there was more and more talk of selling out and moving. The offer price for our place was way down, but at the same time Daddy had found a ninety acre farm in Forsyth county. It had a nice big house on it, along with a big barn and lots of out buildings. It had more and better open land and lots of good timber. All this for five hundred dollars, so we could afford to sell for less.

By the time school started back, there was an air of expectancy mixed with remorse. The crops were gathered as quickly as possible. The older children made no attempt to go back to school; there was too much to do. Elda, R.W., and I were still trekking it the two miles though, to old Weaver School. Then coming home to don our pick-sacks to gather the peas and cotton.

At last the deals were closed. We were sold out. Our move to Forsyth was made certain. We had but to get packed, and everything moved that we could do without. Then just wait until our new place was vacated.

Chapter 20
Teacher's Pet Gone Bad

I was the baby of the family. As could be expected, I was the pet of the family. When I started school at five years old, I was already tutored in counting and saying my a-b-c's. When I got my new primer, I was soon reading all about Baby Ray. I was not, I think, all that smart; but I made the first grade that year as well. All, I'm sure, as a result of my tutoring at home, as well as all the attention I got at school. I loved my teacher dearly; and she, in turn, loved me. As she would brag on me, it would make me want to do more. I was a good kid for the first three years, doing my utmost to get praise from my teacher, as well as at home.

But people change, and I sure changed at school. At recess, and on my way to and from school, I would do anything the older children in the big folks room told me to do. I became a show-out, paying less attention to books and more to meanness. Those poor children that I mentioned that we would share our lunch with, these same children I would throw rocks at and bully them on the way home from school. Some of the big folks would laugh. (I didn't try this when Everett and Edith were along.) I guess the poor children thought that the big boys would back me up, therefore they would run from me. I was ashamed of myself inside, but I wanted to impress the bigger children; so I did it.

My teacher wasn't amused by my antics at school either, I'd purpose not to be naughty anymore, but I kept back-sliding. One day, I

Scrap Cotton

remember, I was having to stay in for something I had done. Another boy, who was one of the meanest in school, had to stay in too. He was angry, very angry. He took the school dipper and beat it all out of shape over the water bucket. So. . . I figured I'd do some meanness too. I found this new book, and began to tear it to bits, stuffing it into the desk, not knowing whose book or desk it was. I was sure I would never be found out, but I was.

Guess what! He was THE meanest boy in school. Also he was a couple of years older than me. The next day he caught me outside alone where he cornered me. He took out his knife and told me, "Bring me thirty cents for the book, or I'll cut your #*%$ *(%$# guts out. " I believed he would do just that, so I told him I would.

This was the greatest trauma of my young life. What would I do? The teacher had already whipped me. Now, if Daddy and Mama found out, Daddy would probably kill me, and I certainly didn't have thirty cents of my own. What to do? For the first time in my life, I didn't want to go to school, but my parents made me go. So, I just made sure that I stayed close to the other children. But eventually, he caught me alone. He was vehement; I had better bring his money.

I knew where a dime was. I opened Mama's machine drawer and looked at it again and again. I knew it was Mama's postage money. But I had to buy this guy off! Or he was going to kill me. I took it. I gave it to him and promised to bring the rest of it soon. But there was no possibility that I could. I stayed in the middle of the other children at recess. I couldn't play ball or fox and hounds with the boys anymore. . . he'd catch me for sure.

Teacher's Pet Gone Bad

It wasn't but a few days until Mama found her dime missing. I helped everyone look for it, reasoning that it had fallen through a crack in the floor. If Mama suspected me, she never indicated she did. Lord, I felt awful.

By now our moving to Forsyth county was imminent. Our place was sold, and Daddy had already paid down on the other. But there seemed to be a bottle-neck in everybody getting moved so that the rest of us could make our move. I listened and inquired diligently as to when we could get to move. That was my only solution, to keep my life. I wouldn't be able to go on keeping safe in a crowd. Sooner or later this boy would get me, and I knew it. Why would anybody be so crazy as to do anything as dumb as destroying a new book? Why was I ever born in the first place?

Needless to say, when it was finally decided that we would move into a vacant house that was near our new home (where we would live until our house was available), I took hope that I would finally be safe. Eight years old, and already a fugitive! How I wished I was still the teacher's pet; but I wasn't. I was a naughty, naughty girl. In fact, I guess I was the 'meanest girl' in school.

Chapter 21
The Transition
1932

Until now, to me moving meant: -bitter cold weather, -a crowded wagon, -two mules to pick their way over the rough road, -me bumping in the wagon bed, -Mama and Daddy bouncing on the spring seat above, braving the cold. There was one thing different this time; I had two cats in a 'toe sack', fighting each other most of the way. (I got a few scratches out of it myself.) Daddy suggested holding them over the side; sure enough, it worked. That biting cold cooled their tempers right away.

None of the rest of the family had a picnic, exactly, on the move. Elda and Edith had gone on the day before with Everett driving the truck. That, granted, was faster; but there was still no cab on the truck. R.W., along with a neighbor who volunteered to help, had the roughest time of all. They drove and/or 'half-drug' the cows the fifteen miles the day before. R.W., according to all reports, almost froze to death, being only eleven years old, with a sizable snow on the ground and slush on the road. None of us, I'm sure, were overdressed for the conditions.

Despite all the hardships, the bigger youn-guns had a great time at our new place that night. It seemed that quite a few of the neighboring youngsters came over to help them unload. Then they frolicked and skated on the frozen snow 'til midnight.

Daddy, Mama and I had stayed at our old place that night with the bare essentials; Mama

The Transition

cooked on the fire place. Everything seemed cozy and special. But the next morning brought remorse. This had been my home, my only home for as long as I could remember. Now it seemed so bleak and cold with the emptiness and dying embers.

Chapter 22
A Christmas Not Too Merry
1932

Our arrival in our new community (a few days before Christmas), found me a worried little girl. I had heard this terrible thing about there being no Santa Claus; and I knew Daddy and Mama had not been to the store. I was afraid to share my thoughts with anyone else, afraid my fears would be confirmed. I just wasn't ready for that yet.

Daddy and Mama did go to the store the next day. I really kept a watchful eye on what they brought in. There was some secrecy and some scolding for being in the way. In fact, R.W. and I were told to go outside and play.

When we were finally allowed to come back in, we asked for a pallet, declaring we wanted to take a nap. We put it down in the back room, between the beds. There were numerous boxes stored under the beds; we both began to feel around in the boxes. I found something that felt like a comb in one box. I withdrew my hand as if it had been burned. I was afraid that I might confirm my deepest fears.

When we had moved into this house, it was only temporary. It was merely a place to stop over until our purchased home could be vacated. The short move to our permanent home a couple of weeks later, was without incident. Not being too much trouble, since we had moved most of our stuff already. Meantime, Mattie Jennings invited us to the school Christmas tree program. Mama told her that I was good at reciting poetry; so I

A Christmas Not Too Merry

was invited to say a Christmas poem at the program.

By now the snow was melted, leaving the roads ankle deep in mud. So, in the mud we walked almost a mile to the school. I had sensibly worn my high-top shoes. (No galloshes now, though we later ordered us some.) Needless to say, our shoes were a mess.

The other children got up with shining patent leather shoes, or at least clean oxfords. I just didn't feel like getting up there at all with my muddy shoes. But I got a special introduction that left me no choice. My poem that I could ordinarily recite without a hitch, just wouldn't come to mind. All I could think about were my shoes and how awful they looked. Now I was hesitating, waiting for the cues to remind me what came next. What a disaster!! Why had I ever gotten up there? Why hadn't Mama brought my Sunday shoes? There was an applause, out of pity, I felt sure.

When Christmas morning finally came, sure enough, Santa had been there. There were goodies in our stockings as usual. There were a couple of oranges and apples, nuts and candies. Then in the foot of one, I found a French-harp. In the foot of the other I found (of all things) a comb. Santa had out done himself.

Chapter 23
Moving Up
1933

It was great to finally get to our new place, and into our new home. The rooms were so large and sealed with beautiful smooth planks. The floors were much nicer, too, with the cracks not nearly so big. But what was so striking were the glass window panes and the beautiful white-washed fireplaces, three of them. The stairs, too, were a novelty, leading to a nice big room on one end and on the other end an unsealed room. This would be what we called our junk room, where we stored things and kept our canned goods. It served as a nice indoor playhouse as well.

There was a front porch that reached almost the length of the house with flower beds and shrubbery in the front yard. On the other side leading to the barn was this huge back porch and an adjoining well shed with a great spreading oak shading that yard and wash place.

Mama had always taken pride in her house and yards. Now she was beaming. I knew she was visualizing the abundance of flowers and rose gardens she later added.

There was a barn or building for every conceivable need. There were two large pastures and fenced lots for every animal or purpose. There would be no new grounds to clear here. There must have been forty or fifty acres already in cultivation. Daddy, of course, already had his eye on acres and acres of timber when he bought the place. He was a happy man.

Moving Up

We younguns were happy, just because everyone else was, I guess. Too, there were lots of youngsters about, and someone was always coming over or stopping by. We were delighted with our new community, but Daddy and Mama were concerned. Edith and Elda had to watch their

Elmo School "Little Folks" Room

step. They were at a vulnerable age they said.

We had this delightful singer and guitarist, Veston Westray, who used to come by on our road on his way to and from his sweetheart's house. They would stop by on occasions, and he would sing and play for us. As far as I can remember, this was my first sight of a guitar. I was fascinated to say the least. I promptly got myself a bucket lid and began to sing and rap on it as if it was a guitar. I even made up my first song called

Scrap Cotton

"Gooshy Feller". (I don't know where I got the title.) The rest of the family thought me a bother, but Mama thought it special, and encouraged me.

There were a few well to do people in the community who had battery powered radios. And, as I understand it, they got plenty of company. I knew it was a big thing when Daddy would light the lantern and we would all walk over to Elmer Westray's house; or Daddy would crank the truck and we would go to Juno Pruitt's house to listen to their radio.

It was all so nice. It seemed we had really moved up in the world.

Chapter 24
Digging In
1933

As soon as we were moved in, Daddy was anxious to get on with the crop preparation. Very soon we were out knocking cotton stalks, cutting down and cutting up the corn stalks. The edges of the field had to be cut back, piled and burned. Daddy and the boys did most of this, but everyone available helped.

Then there were the terraces, and we had plenty of them, for the bulk of our fields were on hillsides. The breaks were mended by piling in rocks, corn stalks and so forth, then thrown up by a shovel. As soon as the ground was thawed and dry enough, the big turning plow was used on all the terraces, throwing them up nice and smooth. It's not all chopping cotton in the spring and picking in the fall. A lot of preparation goes on before the seed goes in.

That spring Daddy planted every conceivable seed, it seemed, that would produce on our land. These were for food we would eat, as well as extra crops that could be turned into cash.

Cotton of course was still king and brought in the lion's share of the cash crop. It also took the lion's share of fertilizer as well. The stables provided a good source of the farmer's fertilizer and our's were piled high with manure. The stables and stalls were dug up and cleaned to the bare earth, then their contents carefully distributed into the open furrows.

The expense of farming, such as the guanno or seed that needed to be purchased, was usually

Scrap Cotton

available to reputable farmers with the promise to pay when the crops were in; but Daddy liked to pay as he went.

We had what was generally termed as a two-horse farm, but in reality we didn't have horses. We had mules which seemed better suited for this type of work.

Everett got to plow Ole Kate who was young and fast stepping. R. W. got Ole Jim who was getting old and slower of step. R. W. was twelve now, and could handle a plow pretty good. That set Daddy free to oversee it all. I was nine and made a pretty good hoe-hand. Then there was Mama, who had to quit early to go to the house to prepare the meals. I guess, between the two of us, we made one good hand to labor beside Edith and Elda.

During that summer, Daddy was sizing up the timber that grew abundantly on our land and was looking ahead to getting a sawmill ready to locate and move in. By that winter when a lot of menfolk were hunting, taking it easy, or finding other work, Daddy and the boys were heading for the woods, felling the trees and getting them snaked to the mill. Daddy was a whiz at finding work for us year-round and he was able to provide work for other people, too, a lot of the time.

R.W. & Floe Ellen

Never waste time or money; that was his motto. He had seen an opportunity to get ahead now. So, we lost no time digging in.

Chapter 25

Spring Cleaning

As soon as it was warm, and the seed was in the ground, and before cotton chopping time, Mama's ritual of spring cleaning began. The bed ticks and the quilts were carried out to sun, while the potash water was brought to a boil in the washpot. Just to be sure no chinches could survive, a little red pepper was added to the boiling water. The bed rails, and even the locks of the head and foot boards were carefully scalded.

Then, with the rest of the furniture being moved around, the scalding of the walls began. There was a real art to doing this. A small utensil was used to throw the water; and it had to be done at a certain angle, so as not to spatter one's self or the furniture. Then lye soap was used in the foot tub to scrub the floors with a new-shuck scrub brush. We had to work fast, and in harmony, so as to get the walls scalded, the floors scrubbed, and then quickly rinsed so as not to let the potash used begin to dry and yellow the wood.

This was all done from room to room. Talk about clean! Though there was an overtone of the potash lingering, to us this was the smell of clean.

Though the fireplaces got white-washed weekly during the winter season, they got one last white-washing during spring cleaning. As soon as flowers, wild or otherwise, were available, a big pot of them were placed in each of the fireplaces.

Mama always replaced the old newspapers on the cookroom shelves with fresh ones as soon as enough papers were accumulated. This was a

Scrap Cotton

slow process, in as much we only received a weekly newspaper and the market bulletin. The old catalogs were used for other purposes.

Of course, we had embroidered doilies for the rest of the house, and embroidered spreads for the beds. If at all possible, we got a new oilcloth for the big kitchen table each spring. Oilcloth cost about thirty cents a yard, and it took more than two yards to spread our table. But Mama could usually squeeze that much out of her butter and egg money.

Once the inside was set in order, Mama would say, "Girls, lets get the hilltop swept." Now that took in a lot of territory! The yards around the house, the wash place, then the walk way to the barn, around the barn and crib, it was all a part of the 'hilltop'. It even included the road in front of the house, all the way to the garage that sat on the other side of the road, just before the land began to fall away on down the road to the fields.

The brush brooms we swept with were made of branches of, preferably, dogwoods. These were bunched and tied together for a handle with the branches spreading out so as to cover a lot of ground. When the grass had grown enough, the big lawn, being the center of the hilltop, had to be slung down with a sling-blade.

The hilltop being now clean, we could get our baths for the weekend. Our bathtub was the biggest washtub we owned. (In the summer, our bathwater was drawn earlier in the day, then it would be placed in the sun to warm. In the winter time we would fill our tub with well water, then add a kettle of hot water.) Then we were ready to sit on the porch to watch the road, if there was nothing else to do.

Chapter 26
Road Watching

Watching the road was a favorite pastime we had. Our road was a quarter of a mile or more off the big road. From the vantage point of our front porch, we could see most of our road, and a good quarter mile of the big road. If we saw someone turn off on our road, we had time to run in the house, comb our hair, change our shoes, or sweep up the hearth (just in case they were, in fact, coming to our house).

A lot of people used our road to walk to the Frogtown community across the creek. Cars didn't use it because the road was just too rough to drive some of the way. The county didn't scrape our road; we had to keep it, and the bridge, up ourselves. When sitting on our front porch, we could see and speak to whoever passed by, or maybe they would have time to stop and chat.

We usually spent our rest period after dinner on the front porch where we could watch for Edmond Moore, our mailman. Being isolated in the country causes one to live in a state of wistful expectancy, looking for anything or anybody from the outside world.

Looking about me, the landscape was now all foreign. A lot of miles seperated us from Mama. She'd do a lot of road watching now, of this I was sure.

Chapter 27

Making the Feathers Fly

Being the baby, Mama kept me close to her. Helping her with all her special projects. Some I liked, like gathering herbs or picking strawberries or gooseberries. But picking the duck's - NO! I dreaded that. I didn't pluck. I held the squawking, kicking duck while Mama plucked. Their down tickled my nose until I'd sometimes let the duck get away while I rubbed it.

Mama said it didn't hurt them. But if not, why the loud protesting quacks with every pluck? Sometimes even relieving their bowels in their usual messy way.

There was another mystery to me. Their pained quack when they mated. Mama being so reserved and private about such things, I was curious that she'd even keep ducks around. They were so blatant in their mating. Unlike chickens, who did so in seconds, the ducks took a minute or more. Quacking from the depths of their lungs as if their pain was unbearable. Then, just like after they had been 'picked' and let go, they'd stretch their necks until they took on the posture of a penguin, flap their wings, swish their tails, then walk proudly away.

Did it hurt? or didn't it? I'll never know, I guess. But their downy feathers sure made a nice cushion between you and a straw tick, as well as pillows fit for a king.

Chapter 28

Monday Washday

Monday washday was principally Mama's day, and my being the youngest, and the most dispensable, it was my job to help from a very early age. Getting things organized was a big ordeal. This, if they had time, Edith and Elda did. Getting the fire under the pot, drawing water, filling the pot, then the tubs. We only had two big tubs, and a little foot tub. This was used to soak the men's dirty socks, or any severely soiled things.

The starch was carefully made while the breakfast stove was still hot. Mama usually had a nickle box of Argo starch, which we used, but sometimes we would be out and have to use flour instead. This was a meticulous job, getting it just right skimming and straining it. The flour starch was bad about sticking to your iron, and sometimes would cause yellow or brown spots on your clothes.

Once the water was hot in the pot, buckets were used to transfer the hot water to the tubs to sufficiently warm the wash-water. The pot was refilled, a piece of lye soap and a dash of 'red devil lye' was added. This water was brought to a boil, ready now for the first load of clothes to be boiled.

Whites were scrubbed, beat with a battling stick, then put in the pot first. There were Sunday white shirts, sheets, Daddy's drawers, as well as union suits, and the guanno sack towels. Then would follow the blue chambry work shirts, dresses, bloomers and the like. Maybe some of these got a quick dip in the washpot. Then came the

Scrap Cotton

menfolks work socks, including the ones we girls wore on our hands for work gloves. Being the uniform gray and white knit, they seemed to stretch with age. After a good battling, they took their dip.

Now it was the heavy wash, since we all wore overalls, except for Mama. They were all soaked, scrubbed, and battled to knock the dirt loose, then dumped into the pot. By the time they were taken out and rinsed well, they were sparkling clean. Somehow, the cleanliness, and varying degree of fading was appealing. Starting out the week on Monday morning in your fresh clothes made you feel very pristine.

Of course, the new overalls worn for Sunday and revival meetings, were, well, "Sundayish" looking and were not rushed into the hot lye water. By the time the overalls were ready for the clothes line, the sheets and the rest of the whites were usually dry, making room for their hanging.

Before the ironing, there was the patching. Mama always patched whether it was a tear or a snag from a tree branch, barb wire, or just plain worn out knees. Each week there was patching to be done. Mama took pride in her washing and patching. "Your menfolk reflect on you," was her firm conviction.

Except when revival meeting's were running, the ironing was not too heavy, thank heaven. We only had one sad iron. Though it held its heat well, one did have to allow for the time it took to heat, and reheat. In the winter, it was set near the embers. In the summer, it was down right torturous having to keep the cookstove going in order to heat it. Mercifully, the stove was in the cookroom, and we ironed in the kitchen. Revivals

Monday Washday

were run in August, and of course, the ironing was multiplied then. We girls for the most part, were out of the fields and able to do the ironing. We were glad we were able to do this. Mama's face got so red from cooking and ironing, we were afraid for her ever-present high blood pressure.

    Clean clothes on Monday was a ritual. Patching was honorable, ragged was a shame. And we didn't go ragged, even if Mama had to patch the patches.

Chapter 29

The White Mud-hole

Everyone, no matter how small, or how big the cracks might be in the house, had one thing in common. In the winter, there was a big crackling fire in the fireplace. The fireplace was white-washed every week. In summer, it stayed white with much less white-washing.

We hadn't had this experience in Pickins county, due to the fact we knew of no white mud-holes there. Here we had the community white mud-hole. It seemed a Mrs. Dooley who owned the property that it was on had long before moved to Atlanta; and no-one thought it wrong to use her mud. The white mudhole was on the side of a branch. One would simply climb down to a sandbar, and dig the chunks of white mud out of the bank. There seemed to be an endless supply.

We would simply get what we could carry in our buckets. Take it home. Then place a few lumps in the white-wash bucket. Add water. Then squish it and stir it until the water was made white with the chalky substance. The sand would settle to the bottom, and the white- wash was ready to be applied with a rag.

A lot of times, it was planned by two, three or more neighbors to go on a specific day and time, meeting there to get the white mud. This could be considered a 'hen party' of a sort, as the women were the ones to go and dig out their choice mud.

I will long remember us, (Mama, Elda, and I), deciding to white- wash our kitchen, which we also used as a sitting room. It was quite large, and the job was overwhelming. We toted mud,

The White Mud-hole

and washed until we ached all over, but we had a white kitchen. A little mottled, yes, but it looked so clean, and much lighter now. It made almost as much difference as the electric lights did when they came.

Chapter 30
Threshing Time

The cotton gin, the grist mill, and syrup mill, were all places you had to take your products for processing. But the sawmill and the wheat threshing machine would come to you. The saw mill was set up in the woods, centrally located within reach of the timber to be sawn. It stayed for weeks or months at one location. The threshing machine made its rounds from one grain farmer to the other. Usually finishing with each farm in a few hours, then moving on to the next.

Lint Harrison at Matt had the community cotton gin, the mobile saw mill, plus the threshing machine. Though the wheat ripened in the early summer, it seemed the weather was always steaming when the wheat was cradled by hand and brought to the barn to wait for the thresher.

That was the day! Wheat, oats, and rye straw flying everywhere into separate heaps. The grain pouring plentifully into containers. Measured, then sacked up for animal consumption, or to be later ground into flour. All of these services were paid for by taking a percentage of the net product.

We much preferred the bleached, self-rising flour bought at the store, but the straw was a necessity. This is what we stuffed our bed-ticks with. We younguns loved to plunge into the straw, grabbing our arms full, and stuffing it into the fresh, emptied, and washed tick. But the biggest thrill of all was to climb half way to the ceiling to get on top of our beds that night. For sure, they would flatten out considerably in a few

Threshing Time

nights. But we loved the feel and the smell of the fresh clean straw ticks, topped with our plump-feather ticks.

Heaps of the remaining straw was piled into the stables for the animals to munch on, and to sleep on. Yep, threshing time was relished, by us kids anyway.

Chapter 31
Hog Killing Time

Hog killing meant me leaving home for the day. It is hard to believe, but I got away with it while I was small. The whole ordeal was repugnant to me. From the rifle shot that was not always exactly on target, the squeals of the hogs, all the blood puddled and running off as the result of a slashed throat. I understood this was necessary so as to drain the blood from the hog, but I still didn't like it. This was sickening!

The smell of the hot water being poured over the body through toesacks, so as to cause the hair to slip out while two or three worked feverishly scraping with their knives. Once all the hair was scraped and the blood washed away, things got a little more bearable.

The 'gamling' stick was thrust through the hocks, then with great effort, the two or three hundred pound hog was hung on the gallows where Daddy gutted it. This wasn't at all pretty either, and the smell was still repulsive. The other organs were saved or discarded, as Daddy saw fit. The liver and heart were saved, but we had no use for the 'lites' or melt. Mama and the girls would keep care of the organs saved for frying or working them up into 'sause' meat.

The head was severed, the skull split, and the brain laid aside to fry. The rest of the head was trimmed and saved for pressmeat. Things looked and smelled better after this.

The not so bloody meat was expertly cut up by Daddy, the fat trimmed for lard. The ham, shoulders, and fatback were hung in the

Hog Killing Time

smokehouse, where a smoldering fire smoked the meat as it drained, as well as kept the flies away. Daddy always salted his meat down the next day. It came out later tasting salty for sure. But wasn't that the way cured meat was suppose to taste?

The lard was rendered in the big washpot, usually lasting into the night. The grinding and mixing of the sausage had to be done next day, when we started the frying and canning of the finished product. Mama always put the fried sausage in jars, then poured the hot grease over it. That way it kept fresh-tasting as long as it lasted.

The backbone, ribs, liver, etc., were shared with a neighbor, usually one who came to help until the heavy work was done. Therefore, he carried a bucket of meat home with him; this was the tradition.

Little wonder I wanted to leave home on these occasions. Besides, it always had to be cold in order to kill hogs, and to me, it seemed it was always windy. Too, Daddy, being an extremely anxious man and short of temper, seemed always to be in a bad mood on hog killing day. It was just not a good time to be home.

Chapter 32
Reason to Hope
1933

We not only had a new and better place to live; we had a new president who gave us renewed hope. It seemed like a new and bright beginning. Daddy, who always kept abreast of things, spoke of it as though a new and better nation was being born. Maybe it was, or maybe I was just beginning to pay attention to things.

When Roosevelt started his famous "Fireside Chats," it gave us another reason to go some place to listen to the radio. People hung onto his every word. He was going to get us out of this stagnant mess that Hoover had gotten us into. FDR was a man of great promise, and he was going to be a man of action.

The terrible stockmarket crash of '29 was making some recovery. Now Roosevelt was going to pick up the pieces, and put them back together. With his "New Deal", people would be back at work with a living wage!

He spoke of the NRA, the WPA, the PWA, the Three C's, and on and on. Certainly speaking of a lot of things that no nine year old could comprehend, but he spoke of helping the farmers. They were the ones who provided the food for our tables and the clothing for our backs; that I could understand; and FDR seemed to understand this basic fact. Here was a president who cared for the farmer, and was placing great value upon him.

Roosevelt cared for the poor. We soon saw proof of that. There were none in our community, but further up the way, I remember seeing two

Reason to Hope

different houses with red crosses in the windows. The cross was placed there so that the relief truck could identify the destitute families that they were to provide necessities for. (The American Red Cross was, of course, the benefactor, yet we felt it was prompted by our new president.) Some people, who I suppose were not near starvation, talked of how disgraceful it was to have a red cross in the window. But I can understand, now, how when your family is hungry and cold, pride could be swallowed.

Mama reminded us how Roosevelt had quoted scripture; how that if "one has not charity, he is nothing." I now know this was from the thirteenth chapter of I Corinthians. Surely he was a Christian, and a God fearing man. People liked that.

Getting down to where we lived.... Maybe we didn't have the best of clothes to wear, but we didn't go hungry. We never did, not even during the depth of the Great Depression. Being farmers, perhaps, gave us the edge over people on public works. We knew how to work. We were not afraid of work; and we had the will and determination to persevere. We knew how to take care of the things we were blessed with. We knew how to do without, not that it was always easy. We learned how to parch and grind rye to make a substitute

Mama & Daddy

Scrap Cotton

for coffee. Mama learned to dry and powder tobacco leaves to replace her Bruton snuff. She learned how to make a syrup to pour over shredded tobacco leaves, then dry it out in the oven to replace Daddy's Prince Albert pipe tobacco.

As I have indicated before, we were inspired to persevere, for the present, so as to have a better tomorrow. Now Roosevelt was inspiring, and promising just that - a better tomorrow. New programs were soon being put into operation all over.

Cotton, due in part to a glutted market, was bringing little more than six cents per pound. But Roosevelt was promising that by compulsory measures to reduce the amount of cotton being grown, prices could be brought to ten cents per pound. He put into effect a program that actually paid the farmer not to plant as much as the year before. This was called subsidizing. Eventually, we were paid to plow up a part of the cotton already planted on our alotted acres.

Less work for more money. This surely was a good reason to hope.

Chapter 33

Noticing a Difference

Churches were plentiful here, but their mode of worship was somewhat different than where we came from, though not many miles removed. Daddy was quick to point out the differences, but Mama was just happy to be going to church. We younguns were happy, too; perhaps for a different reason, though.

It didn't take long to notice a difference in the people. Here, most of the church-going people dressed better than we did, and some were downright biggity. At Corinth, there had definitely been some better dressed, yet we all intermingled. Edith and Elda were quick to pick up on this, and began to bemoan the situation to Daddy. Daddy was totally unimpressed, saying, "You all are as good as anybody else, and don't forget it! They probably have everything they own on their backs, anyway. And, yes," he would say, "We do have some ten cent millionaires." But he told us that what was important was to pay your debts, and keep some money in your pocket.

Mama was much more understanding. She promised to try and get Daddy to allow us more money. Meanwhile, we could cut some corners of our own. We would cut back on our egg eating. Maybe slip in a little more cotton seed meal to the cows and pull them some choice weeds and pea vines, all of which would make for richer milk, producing more butter.

You could buy a yard of print cloth for seven cents; organdy, pique, or georgette material for a little more; enough lace to trim a dress for a pit-

Scrap Cotton

tance; a card of pretty buttons for a nickle. Then with a little expertise at the machine, you had a new dress for thirty or forty cents. One could always borrow a different pattern, or even buy one for a dime.

But, of course, the everyday necessities had to be bought first. There was fifteen cents for a pound of coffee, twenty-five cents for four pounds of sugar. Soda was a nickle; kerosine for the lamps was a dime a gallon. A ball of thread for patching and quilting was a nickle; a large spool of mercerized thread for the machine was a dime. A small spool of colored thread for dresses was a nickle. All of these things, Mama was expected to buy with her barter. If there was less than a nickle left over, we could have it for candy and chewing gum. Anything above a nickle was taken in a 'due bill'. A few of these could add up to enough to buy material for a dress.

All of this sounds easy. But, when you consider eggs brought only eight cents per dozen; butter, ten cents per pound; a frying size chicken brought ten cents per pound; but a rooster or an old hen wasn't worth more than eight cents per pound. So, it took a lot of barter to buy these things.

Daddy would go to Gainsville, and buy the heavy things like a hundred or so pounds of sugar for canning and making jelly. He got this for four dollars per hundred pound. He'd buy our tennis shoes for summer field wear for forty-eight cents a pair. Overalls for eighty-nine cents. He'd get several pounds of dried beans for the winter months. He'd pay cash for all of this. Then he would charge our lard (if we bought any), plow lines, plows, medicines, and things of that sort.

Noticing a Difference

Then pay up in the fall when the crops were in. Our charges would run from forty to sixty dollars each year. He considered this with the expenses of making a crop.

The things Daddy deemed necessary included buying us an outfit in the spring and again in the fall. This was enough; he saw no need for anything more. Daddy was one of a kind; we knew that. He was obsessed with getting ahead, and making money was all he wanted to talk about.

Mama was one of a kind, too; she was just too religious, we felt. Mama was afraid someone was going to mention something about sex. (This was a subject that was treated, by her, like Santa Claus in front of small children.) It just wasn't talked about. If someone mentioned their period, or about someone 'getting big' or 'being caught', she'd turn red as a beet. I would scoot fast, if it sounded like a conversation was leading in this direction. If someone started to tell an off colored joke, she'd squirm pitifully.

Most other younguns got to go to dances or 'musics', as we called them, when the young men of the community who made music, would meet at someone's house and play while everyone else danced; but we weren't allowed to dance. Little wonder we began to lie early, saying there would be no dancing in order to get to go. When other young people came by to get us to go some place with them, most often we didn't get to go. Consequently, they just quit coming by for us.

All the people who came to see us when we first moved here, began to dwindle. We blamed Daddy and Mama. It was hard being different.

Chapter 34
Shopping Adventure

Before our first crop on our new farm was in, Esther wrote us a letter wanting to know if Edith could come down for the winter and keep her kids. In reality, she needed a maid, having her own hands full with her two older children, and now a third was due. She would soon be going back to work. She agreed to pay Edith three dollars per week, and Edith would cook, wash, and clean while keeping her three children. We all waited with baited breath while Mama broached Daddy on the subject. To all of our relief, and surprise, he said she could go, provided she came home in the spring in time to help with the crop. This was agreed upon. Edith stayed home until the bulk of the gathering was in; Elda and I would get all the scrap cotton this year. Of course, this was merely a token, but well worth braving the cold to gather.

Daddy took us to Gainsville and bought us sweaters and shoes and such as he thought we needed. I will never forget the trip. We had ridden in on the load of cotton in the back of the truck. Before one bit of shopping was done, we had to wait until the cotton could be ginned, baled, and sold right on the spot. Then, with the money in his pocket, we all went shopping for our winter clothes. (This being the last bale of the year, and our bills being paid.)

As you can imagine, all this took the whole day. Mama had brought us some stuffed biscuits, which we consumed before we shopped. Then on our last stop at McClelland's Five-and-Dime,

Shopping Adventure

Daddy bought us some hot mixed nuts, which we all shared. Then for the long, cold trip home. We had dug us a nest in the cotton on the way over, but now we had not much to shield us from the cold. We backed up against the truckbed, just behind Daddy and Mama. This knocked off most of the wind; Mama and Daddy had only the windshield to protect them. About half-way home, I grew deathly sick. The first thing I thought of was, "It must have been the hot nuts." But really, it was probably because I was riding backwards. Whatever the cause, I have never eaten hot nuts again. My great adventure to the big city was almost ruined.

Chapter 35
Indian Lore

Our farm had been occupied by the Cherokee Indians until 1836, when they were forced out. Small relics lured me to keep an eye to the ground each time the fields were plowed. There was a chance of at least a piece of a relic being unearthed.

The fact that I was something of a dreamer, and having an inquiring mind, contributed to my reputation of being a slow poke, if not a little lazy. But to me, I was just enriching my life by the things I found, or anticipated finding. I found many pieces of broken pottery, arrowheads, or parts thereof.

I collected many objects carved of stone. I found a couple of, what appeared to be, carved colorful and transparent stones, which I later identified as amethyst. One being about five inches long by an inch and a half wide. They were somewhat rough on the bottom, but the tops were like polished glass.

A couple of miles beyond our house were these boulders, one being especially huge, having many Indian carvings on it. These lay in full view of the road. Elda and I used to stop and re-examine them each time we walked that way, believing there had to be a message on them. We often wondered if they told of buried treasure.

Sure enough, it turned out the owner of this property had been approached in 1932 by a man from Canton, Georgia, wanting permission to do some sort of surveying to see if there was in fact a buried treasure nearby. The owner, Mr. Rester

Indian Lore

Groover consented. The two of them walked and surveyed until they found the spot indicating the treasure. As it happened it was just about nightfall, so they agreed to meet back there at nine o'clock the next morning to start their digging.

When Mr. Groover got there, the other man didn't show. Becoming worried, he walked to the sight and found only an empty hole. A lawsuit followed, the perpetrator admitted he had taken twenty thousand dollars in dust (at a price of thirty-two dollars an ounce), seventeen thousand in nuggets and coins. He admitted to this; there could have been much more. But the judge ruled, finder's keepers, since it was a buried treasure. Mr. Groover got nothing, except he still had the engraved boulders.[1]

---

1   The huge boulder bearing the indian markings can be found on the campus of the University of Georgia in Athens.

Chapter 36

Gold!!!

A farm without a branch or two on it just wouldn't be a farm. We had a creek and a couple of branches on our property. One branch in each pasture, and a creek through the "bottom" lands. In one of the branches, R.W. and Everett busied themselves and built us a swimming hole. A really good one with a diving board. It was six feet deep at the lower end. By sliding down this big smooth rock, you could land in about three feet of water at the end where the water backed up.

Young folks from miles around came to enjoy it. Most everyone wore their overalls in swimming, like we did. But some of the girls wore bathing suits, and Mama didn't like it at all.

Just a little way up from the swimming hole, R.W and I were exploring the branch one day. We noticed these bright-looking grains of something glistening in the water. When we traced it to its source, we found a small bank of it. "Gold!!", was our first inclination. It was so very bright and shiny, just like gold. It had to be!

We salvaged some of it in our hands, and ran all the way home. Mama looked at it and agreed, it did look like gold. But she was pessimistic, "It could be fool's gold." We had heard of that too, but maybe.....

Elda and Edith went back with us. "It is gold, and we are rich," was their opinion. How were we going to find out for sure? Daddy was gone off for the day. We could hardly wait for him to get home. He would know what to do. Meanwhile, of

Gold!!!

course, we couldn't let anyone know what we had found nor where we had found it.

Daddy wasn't that impressed. It took a week or more to get him over there to see the source. Still, he wasn't impressed. "Real gold wouldn't be that shiny," he insisted. He wouldn't do a thing. Our fever soon cooled, but the possibility still lingered.

At times when we were blue, Elda and I would go over there and just sit and watch as the water continued to grasp and mingle with "our gold" as it washed on down the stream. Thousands of dollars could be just washing away! We thought about it; we talked about it; and we dreamed about it.

We gathered some if it, and kept it anyway. Someday, someway, we had to know for sure. Was it Gold?[1]

---

[1] It would be years later after we had left home, that we took a bus from Griffin to Atlanta, where we carried the dust to the capital to be analyzed. We found out it was not gold after all. We carried it back to Griffin with us and reluctantly poured it out. It was gone, but not forgotten.

Chapter 37
A Sticky Business
1934

One of the crops Daddy planted was sorghum cane. Harvesting this was the one thing worse than corn fodder pulling. We had to strip it from towering top to bottom. We didn't salvage the fodder, so it was dropped on the ground, supposedly helping to enrich the soil.

Once the cane was stripped, two or three people would go ahead, each grabbing four or five stalks in each hand. The cutter would follow with a mowing blade, giving a jerky motion, cutting stalk by stalk. While the first holder carefully laid their cane down, the cutter was going smoothly along cutting for number two, then number three. By this time the first person was holding again, and so on. It was teamwork, indeed. (Everyone did their share of sweating. Though it was September, the heat could be sweltering.)

Once the cane was neatly piled along the rows, we brought in the two-horse wagon. Either Mama or Daddy would drive the wagon along, while the rest loaded it for the homeward trip. There were several of these trips since we not only grew cane for our ownselves, but always had syrup for sale.

Once the canes were brought to the barn, it was unloaded close by our syrup mill. (The mill had been a bonus with our farm when we bought it.) A few other people brought their cane for us to make their syrup, which we did for a portion of the syrup. But most people took their cane to

A Sticky Business

Anderson Sexton who had a syrup mill of longstanding.

I'll always remember the first time I got to take a real hand in making syrup. Up until then, I only got to feed some cane into the press, where the juice was extracted and run into the holding barrel before being dispensed into the first cooking pan. The 'pummies', or the crushed cane stalks, were piled high. They were later hauled away and put in the ruts of the road, or used to stop washes where-ever.

Everett was in charge of the syrup making this year. He said, "Smokehouse, (his favorite nick-name for me) do you reckon you could help me this time?"

I got real choked up and replied, "Me?"

"Yeah," he said. "Just you and me are going to make this batch."

I felt ten feet tall! And never so good in my life. You can well imagine I did everything just as I was told to do, never minding the terrible heat coming off that boiling juice and the rock furnace. Me and my big brother were doing this thing together.

We had a good market for the syrup that we had left over after we filled our own fifty gallon barrel. We put some in a barrel to dispense by the quart, or as much as the customer would need. Then we bought twenty shiny, new syrup buckets at a dime each. We filled and capped them. Then it was off to Marble Hill for Daddy and Everett, where they sold the syrup getting a good price of sixty cents per gallon. Imagine my delight, when Everett later brought back the report that folks were saying this was the best syrup they had ever eaten.

Scrap Cotton

Seems we had left it just long enough in each partition of the pan, and had skimmed it well to take out the bitterness, and then, at just the right moment, had drained the syrup into the barrell, when the color was right, the consistancy ideal, and the taste superb. Not everybody had our expertise.

This, by the way, would be Everett's last year at home before he went to Griffin to work in the cotton mill. But my big brother had recongnized that I had capabilities. I was a responsible person now.

Chapter 38

The Dusty Miller

When Egbert lived at the River, he had a three fold job. He farmed, he ran the water-powered grist mill, as well as being the boatsman back and forth across the river. People would come to the river bank, and holler until Egbert would hear them. He would come row them across to the other side, then back to his bank, or visa- versa.

There was just this one crossing, several miles away from the bridge that spanned it further down the river. This, as a matter of fact, was the route horses and vehicles had to take, but people on foot chose this shorter way.

The picture is still vivid in my mind. The first time Edith, Elda, R.W. and I went to spend the night with him, the big and muddy river was awesome looking. Had I not wanted so badly to visit him, I think I would have turned around and made them take me back home. When he came rowing across for us, I cautiously stepped into the boat for my very first boatride. I hardly breathed until we reached the other side.

Once we got to his house, it was fascinating, exploring the old mill. This was a first for me as well. R.W. and I scouted up the mill race as far as we dared. Little wonder they called it a race. The walled-in water was very swift as it plunged down to and over the big wheel that turned the big stones inside.

Egbert was grinding some meal when we had interrupted him with our hollering at the river. He was comical looking with the fine meal settled

Scrap Cotton

on his hat and clothes. He sure looked the part of a 'dusty miller'.

Chapter 39

The Family Dwindles

By the fall of '34, things were really looking up for Daddy. He had sufficient family members to handle things. He was really getting ambitious about all he would be turning out. Too ambitious, I would say, or too assuming.

Everett was twenty-one, and was dating a good bit. He wanted more money of his own; and didn't like being told what to do and what not to do. His attitude clashed with Daddy's personality. Friction increased, and Everett left home.

The cotton mills were now in full production, so he went to Griffin. He got a job in the mill where Esther and Clarence worked, boarding with them.

Edith didn't go back to work for Esther that fall; I guess since Everett was gone, she felt she should stay home. R.W. was now thirteen, so he stepped up to try and fill Everett's place, except he couldn't drive the truck. So, Daddy sold it to Egbert. He then hired his lumber hauled. At least the women in the family were not asked to go into the woods this time. (I guess Daddy figured he had better loosen up a bit.)

That fall he gave us all ten dollars each out of the last bale of cotton, took us to Gainseville, and told us to buy what we needed. Wow! What a shopping experience. We got shoes, $1.98 a pair. $1.98 bought us a really nice dress, seventy-nine cents for a slip, unmentionables for a dime, mercerized socks for fifteen cents, a hat for a dollar. Edith and Elda got handbags and some makeup: 'tange' rougue, lipstick, 'mabeline', face cream,

Scrap Cotton

and powders. Arid and perfume for a dime each. I got a dress, socks and shoes, a nice sweater for $1.98, some beads, some ebroidery hoops, and embroidery thread (three cents a skein). (Mama was already teaching me to embroider.) Then they gave us a big box of dusting powder, just for being among the first in the store that day.

I had never had so much money in my life. It was great! But I would rather have my family back together. Egbert and his family, although he hadn't been living with us, had gone to Griffin as well. I missed them all.

Chapter 40

The Funnies and Chocolate Cake

John and Inez Stubblefield and their two children had moved to our community from Atlanta during the Great Depression. In fact, they had moved into one of our houses. They were a novelty to us, being city folks. It was a lot of fun, acquainting them with a farm and its peculiarities.

They had something that was awesome to me, as well, a big luxurious "hupmobile." One day, Daddy got John to carry us to the dentist at Marble Hill, where I was to have a jaw tooth extracted. On the way, sitting in the big soft seat, we would spring up and down at every bump in the road. Daddy caught me bouncing when indeed there had been no bump. Everyone laughed. After that I bounced only when the car did.

After we moved to Forsyth county, they moved there as well, not too far from us. They would drive somewhere every Sunday morning, (to Rosco Grogan's store, I assume), to pick up an Atlanta Constitution.

One Sunday morning, Daddy said I could go over there with him. I was elated. I loved to visit and especially loved to read the 'Funnies': Dick Tracy, Little Orphan Annie, Mutt and Jeff, Brenda Star and all the rest. I read them eagerly. When Daddy said it was time to go, I begged to stay. Inez encouraged him to let me stay for dinner. He agreed; I could stay that long.

Mildred was somewhat older than me, a teenager at least. She had her friend, Hazle Martin over that day, and I'm sure I was a thorn in

Scrap Cotton

their sides. I would have been going home soon after dinner, but Inez started baking a chocolate cake. It smelled so good cooking, I couldn't bring myself to leave. I stayed. Finally, when the cake was served, somehow, I just forgot to go home. I kept staying. Finally, Inez said, "Floe Ellen, its going to be getting dark soon. Don't you think you had better go now?" My heart almost failed me. What in the world had I done? Staying all day? I knew I was in big trouble.

On the way home, I concocted all kinds of excuses. Like, I had fallen and knocked myself out. I came up on this copper wire that had been unwound from an old battery.....maybe if I told Daddy I had gotten tangled up in this wire... No, no, no. None of these things would hold up. I was just in trouble, and that's all there was to it.

I was in trouble alright. It was just about night when I got home. Maybe it would be too late for Daddy to get a hickory, but it wasn't. He had already cut it, and it was standing by the fireplace. Mama just shook her head in disbelief. "Why? Floe Ellen, why?"

"Inez cooked a chocolate cake, Mama." I pleaded. She just shook her head, feeling sorry for me, I'm sure. Daddy was coming in from the barn, now.

Chapter 41
Christmas '34

Everett came home on a visit for Christmas, his and Daddy's differences evidently cooled. He came through on the old truck with Egbert. Though Egbert had built something of a cab on the truck, they were all but frozen. As long as I live, I won't forget that Christmas. I guess it was the best Christmas of my life.

When we picked and sold our scrap cotton that year, I saved the seventy cents I had gotten for my part. I was able to sit down with our Sears & Roebuck catalog, and pick out everyone a present. I found colorful washcloths for five cents each. They were pink, blue, yellow, and green. The women folks, as well as myself, got yellow. The two nephews got green. My nieces got pink. The men folk got blue. I was so proud. Mama did remind us these were washcloths, not washrags as we usually referred to them. For that was just what they were in that day, rags used to wash with.

I felt awfully good giving my gifts, but this Christmas, I got the most wonderful gift of my life. Everett unloaded the most beautiful bike we had ever seen. Second hand, of course, but red, white and shiny with green and red Christmas roping woven between the spokes of the wheels.

R.W. and I took turns learning to ride on the solidly frozen ground. R.W. was getting the lion's share of turns until Daddy, Egbert, and Everett asked him to go someplace with them. They were gone for three or four hours. When R.W. got back, there was not a dent in the ground or either of

Scrap Cotton

the three chimneys that I had used to push off from, but there was a lot of skin gone off my extremities. None the less I was riding that bike, and pretty good too!

Everett must have been as proud of giving us that three dollar bike as I was of everybody's washcloths. Washcloths were great, but never in my life had I had such a grand possesion. Even if it was in co- ownership with R.W.

Chapter 42
The Magic of Town
1935

The winter that Edith went to Griffin, she had come home with nice clothes and a permanent. Everett and Egbert were there this winter. Everett working in a cotton mill, while Egbert had rented a little store and produce market. Egbert would write to say how well he was doing, and we were so proud that he was able to provide for his family better. When Everett came home with R.W.'s and my new bike, money jingling in his pocket, and passing out chewing gum, we knew he was doing alright.

We were later to discover his store bought toothbrush, and Pepsodent toothpaste. We were fascinated by his aftershave lotion as well, and would have used some of it ourselves, but the scent would have given us away. His toothbrush and toothpaste was different. Elda and I just had to try it. Wow! I'll never forget the zing of that Pepsodent toothpaste. As for a toothbrush, the only things we had ever had was a mop chewed on the knot-end of a blackgum twig, or the corner of a washrag with Arm-n-Hammer baking soda. I'm sure, had we asked, he would have shared his toothpaste. But as for using his brush, he would have balked at that.

It just seemed to me, everyone who worked in town had so many things. There just had to be something magical about town, but tragedy came.

None of us had ever had measles. But shortly after Christmas, Egbert wrote that Harley, his oldest son, had the measles. He was very sick

Scrap Cotton

with them, and had developed pneumonia. A couple of days later after we received the letter, we saw two cars coming on our road that night. Mama began to cry, "Harley's dead. Harley's dead." And he was. They were bringing him home for burial. I was crushed. Harley had been my buddy. I remembered him being born, and how close we had been to him the first five years of his young life. His had been the first family death I had witnessed. It was, oh, so heart rending to see him put in the ground in that little Corinth cemetary, and to leave him there at the tender age of six.

Town had not been all that kind after all. Its magic almost lost its luster.

Chapter 43
A New Car?
1935

When Egbert and LouAnna had decided to give up farming and move to Griffin, he needed a truck to move on. Daddy offered to sell him our truck. Since Everett was gone, he was having to hire his lumber hauled, anyway; so Egbert bought it.

Now a wagon was our only mode of transportation. To ride to church in a wagon now, was even beneath Mama's dignity. So we went to church very little that winter. Then, only when we could get a way to ride with someone else. Daddy said maybe we would get a new car.

Come spring, Wilson Turner began his visits again. He would bring first one car, then another. One was a black shiny, almost new car. We kids were elated. I remember Elda and I going out, sitting in it, admiring its pretty interior, springing up and down in the plush seats, while imagining riding up to church in it. Wilson really encouraged Daddy to buy this one. But Daddy turned it down, to our utter dismay.

Then one day, Wilson drove up in a gray, boxy-looking chevy. Even though the seats were plush with the nice velour upholstery, drab was the way one would have to describe it. "It runs as smooth as silk," Wilson encouraged. It was nice and well taken care of, yet it was a '28 model, seven years old!

We had high hopes of a new car, or at least a nice black shiny one. Now this! Elda said she just wasn't going to ride in it, and we didn't on a

Scrap Cotton

lot of occasions. We'd walk while Mama and Daddy rode, if he would permit it.

It rode so much better than the old truck we had had. Mama was happy, but we weren't. A new car....Baaaaa.... we just couldn't win.

Chapter 44

Canton Woman

While Roosevelt's plan for Recovery was now working, we were still not exactly rolling in money from our labors. Employment was up, so we girls hit up on a plan where we could better ourselves financially. We talked at length with Mama about it. We wanted us to move to Canton where the older children could get employment in the cotton mill there. Daddy could get a job, too.

Our plan had good possibilities. When R.W. and I got big enough, we could go to work as well. All together we could have a great income. Each of us making twelve or thirteen dollars a week. Mama was impressed somewhat, but not that optimistic. She recounted as to how she used to think a cotton mill was not a respectable place for girls to work, but then there was Esther working in one. So, maybe they had changed.

Anyway, Daddy would never consent. He was a farmer, always had been, always would be, so we may as well forget it. None-the-less, we broached the subject to Daddy. To our surprise he didn't give an emphatic "NO!". He just reminded us, "What would happen when you all get older and start 'marrying off'? What then?"

We girls had seen a ray of hope, and we wouldn't let go. We continued to discuss it with Mama. We began to chide while we invisioned living in town. Why! Mama could be a lady of leisure, wearing pretty dresses everyday, as we imagined town folk wore. Mama picked up on the vision and would smile. "Show us how you would walk," we urged her. Mama would tilt her head,

Scrap Cotton

hold her shoulders back a little more, carry her left hand limply in front of her, with her little finger flirted up. Then walk a little prissy, a little out of character for Mama, yes, but Lord this was how it should be. Mama deserved so much more than the drab life she had. We delighted to see her playing the role, anyway.

Meantime, we'd just have our own secret joke. This lifted our spirits many times. Daddy never knew what we meant when we called Mama "Canton woman" How could we let our dreams die?

Chapter 45
Another Tragedy
1936

Next fall, Edith went back to Griffin. This time she worked for Egbert and Everett. They had rented another store, and still hauled produce for other stores as well. They were making it good, but tragedy struck again. They were having flu, one after the other. Then LuAnna, Egbert's wife, got pneumonia. Just one year and two days from Harley's death, LuAnna died, leaving Egbert with an eight month old baby and two other small children.

When Harley died, they brought him through in a car. But Egbert, having no insurance, had Everett to bring LouAnna through on the truck. The rest came by car. The weather was frigid, and Everett was frozen half to death when he arrived.

It was, oh, so sad and pitiful for Egbert and his small children. We were all willing to do whatever we could. Egbert said that he had had enough of Griffin, and would never go back. Daddy told him to go get his things, and bring them to our house, so Mama could take care of the baby and the other children. Egbert took him up on the offer. Edith finished the winter working for Esther, and Everett joined the Three C's.

Daddy had never been a public drunk, since he always brought his bottle home. We kids, and perhaps Mama too, wished he didn't come home when he was drinking, for he was to be dreaded some of the time. We kids scooted when he did bring his bottle home, and Mama did all she

Scrap Cotton

could to please. He had been sober, for the most part, for several years. But this winter, he went on a binge.

Then one day, he took a wagon whip to R.W. and me because we were playing instead of shucking corn. Egbert interceded, and that was the last of Egbert living with us. Daddy said he had to go, and go he did, with those kids and a snow on the ground. Mama and us children were devastated. Egbert found him a house, and an older woman to watch the kids while he worked at whatever he could find.

By late the next summer, he had met and married another wife. We all breathed a sigh of relief. Death had taken a terrible toll on his family and it had been felt by us all.

Chapter 46
Brass Tacks

Daddy wouldn't permit us to play basketball at school. It "wore out too much shoe leather", and was not "akin to an education." He didn't "send us to school to play"; he "sent us to learn." Of course, we played ball anyway, but boy did we watch the road for Daddy to pass, at recess, or on the lunch hour. Sometimes we actually went to other schools to compete, but felt as though we were taking our lives into our own hands to do so.

I say 'we' went, but I only got to play one time. That was because another one of the regular girls was unable to go that day. Boy, did I feel great, especially after we won! Elda and R.W. were always on the team. But between my bunion and my natural inability to run, I never made it.

Talk about a crisis, we really had one at this one game. R.W. and a big fellow on the opposing team both jumped for a rebound, and collided in mid-air. They came down with a sickening thud. R.W. was hurt bad. He had to come out with his arm hanging limp. He just wasn't the type to admit pain, but he was as white as a sheet and unsteady on his feet. We all knew he needed a doctor, but no way was he going to let Daddy know. For sure Daddy would find out that he had been playing ball when he hurt it.

So, afterwards, at his insistence, Elda and I would take turns pulling on his arm, trying to 'fix it' or set it. We covered for him every way we could; doing his chores around the house, cutting the wood and all. As well as working extra hard in the fields, so one of us could slip away and

Scrap Cotton

plow for him. Fortunately, it was a slow time of the year. There wasn't anything pressing. Elda and I were picking peas, and he was plowing under some ground cover so as to enrich the soil for next year.

He suffered a lot, but we didn't even tell Mama. She probably would have felt obligated to tell Daddy. It was several weeks, before he got relief. It was a few years later, when he had hurt it again (working this time), Daddy carried him to the doctor for x-rays. Sure enough, he had broken his collar bone. And wouldn't you know, the doctor found an old break, that, for the life of him, R.W. couldn't remember when and how it had been broken. The doctor was skeptical, but didn't press the issue.

Daddy just couldn't understand how we wore out our winter shoes so quickly. The summer didn't demand too much on our shoes. We either went barefoot, or wore old tennis shoes, and we could wear them on and on. The uppers were soon full of holes, but the bottoms were practically indestructible. When our winter shoes wore through on the bottom, Mama was our cobbler. She could extend their lives over and over, and make them last through the winter.

When a pair of shoes was completely worn out, they were not thrown away until every salvagable part was used up. We kept a half-bushel basket for the worn out shoes sitting against the wall on the back porch beside the shoe last. The tongues of the shoes were usually used to make flip and sling-shot pockets, being too thin for shoe repair. The sides of the shoes, being the least worn, were cut out in shapes for the repair job, and were used to half-sole the needy pair, or

Brass Tacks

build-up a heel that might have been 'run over'. Now and then, Daddy would buy a sheet of leather, especially for half-soling shoes. But this was used on the menfolks heavier shoes, being thick as it was.

Mama would do a neat job trimming around the edges with Daddy's sharp knife until it didn't show too much on the sides. But boy, those tacks! She had short tacks for the soles, long ones for the heels. She would try and hammer them against the last, until the sharp end didn't stick you. But try as she would, when you stepped on a rock, the tack would press against your foot, even though it was bradded. You just got used to the bottom of your feet being sore.

I don't care how well sewn your shoes looked when they were new, they always, somehow, managed to break loose where the back and the front came together and the tongue started. When this happened, Mama had to sew it with wire, and then tie it off on the outside. This made the shoe look very bad, tacky to say the least. It almost made you want to quit playing ball.

Chapter 47
A Lesson Well Learned
1936

Before it burned, we enjoyed a two-room school house. There was the big folks' room for the fifth through the eighth grades. The little folks room was for the first through the fourth grades. I was in the seventh, and sure felt my stuff. We got to go to basket ball games to play and, sometimes, to watch the boys play.

One day, we had planned to go watch the boys play, but Mr. Ford couldn't line up another car to carry us girls. To say that we were disappointed was an understatement. We were furious! We watched while Mr. Ford and six boys crowded in and onto Mr. Ford's 1932 Sport Roadster. They were packed all over each other in the rumble seat. Of course, there was no way we could have gone with them in his car.

This was bad enough. But to add insult to injury, he instructed us to go into Miss Katie's room with the little kids. My Lord! It had taken forever to get out of the little folks' room, and now to go back in there was just too much! Me and two of my best friends decided we wouldn't stay in there. So, we simply got up and walked out.

We walked down into the 'girls' woods' where we sat and talked for a while. We found somebody's old lunch poke; then picked some rabbit tobacco, and rolled us some cigarettes. But we had no matches. We couldn't think of a way to get a match, so.. so much for that. We would go back to the school house and get the other basketball and shoot some goals. But, Miss Katie wouldn't

A Lesson Well Learned

let us have it. We swore at her! She begged us to come back in; instead, we defiantly walked away.

We were bored, there just wasn't anything to do. Then we began to pick up rocks and pretend to shoot goals, banging the backboards. We knew we were disturbing the other children inside, but we didn't care. Miss Katie came out one last time and implored us to come inside. I noticed she was crying and I felt ashamed. I didn't curse at her anymore, but one of the girls swore at her and said a lot of terrible things. I just didn't have the stomach for it; I felt sick. Three o'clock came. Mr. Ford and the boys still weren't back, so we all went home.

The next day, Mr. Ford called us three girls up in front of the class. Did we want ten licks each, or did we want to write Miss Katie an apology, one thousand times each? He had never whipped one of us girls before, but we had seen him lay the hickory on some of the boys now and then (usually for cursing or fighting). We didn't want him to get hold of us. So, we told him we would write the apologies.

The apology was so long, we couldn't get it all on one line. I was worried sick as to where I would get all that extra paper. Daddy knew how long a tablet should last, so I was 'daresent' to waste it. I rummaged the trash bucket. I tore up paper pokes. I slipped into the brownpaper wrapping we saved at home when we got goods wrapped from the store. One thousand times made for a lot of writing, an awful lot of writing. When we complained to Mr. Ford, he made a bargain with us. Five hundred times and five licks. One of the girls had her five hundred. So, next day she came with about three layers of clothes

Scrap Cotton

on and reported she was ready for her five licks. Despite her padding, I noticed she winced with every lick. Gee.......

Next day, the other girl stood up and took hers. Ole slow poke me barely made it by the next day. But I didn't have all the extra clothes on, Mama would have caught me for sure, before or after school. I couldn't take the chance. I took my five licks, and I'm sure there were five whelps on my back, but I felt relieved it was over.

But, Mr. Ford felt that we had another obligation. Miss Katie was due more than a written apology. We were to verbally apologize before both rooms. He pulled back the curtain at the end of the partition, and called Miss Katie to the opening. He had us march up to her and tell her we were sorry we had been disrespectful.

I, in order, was the last one to face her. When we took our licks, neither of us cried. But now I was blubbering like a six year old. I had never said, "I'm sorry" in my whole life. It just wasn't in my vocabulary. I thought I would choke on the words. Not that I wasn't sorry, I was! In fact, I had an overwhelming urge to hug her neck and tell her I loved her, but I was too soppy for that. At last, I said the words, and was proud that I had.

From that day forward, when I have done anything wrong, it is the easiest thing in the English language to say, "I'm sorry."

The damage Mr. Ford did to me was on my back, and it felt good once it quit hurting. The damage another teacher did to me when I was in the fourth grade would last a lifetime. It was Valentine's Day, and Daddy had bought me some valentines, enough to give one to all the children

A Lesson Well Learned

in my room. I felt good. But, with my ongoing spelling difficulty, I spelled 'Nellie Kate' wrong. My teacher held it up for the room to see, ridiculing me. I had spelled her name C-a-t-e. The children laughed, and my day was ruined. I had done nothing wrong. I had simply made a mistake. Yet the damage she did to me still hurts when I recall it.

With Ford Phillips and Katie Harris, I had disregarded authority. I had deliberately disobeyed them, and I deserved the punishment I got. I felt no animosity toward anyone. Instead, my soul felt cleansed, and my self esteem was still intact. In fact, I can laugh about it now.

Chapter 48
Stepping Out In Style

Edith came home in the spring, just as she had promised. Boy, what a thrill! It was good to have her back. She looked so pretty and sophisticated in the new clothes she had managed to buy. And, surprise of surprises, she had Elda and I new complete outfits. She bought Elda a pretty pink dress, a pink hat, and pink mercerized socks, along with white shoes and white bag. She brought me a pretty blue ruffled dress, with a knit blue and white striped tam, new white shoes, and pretty blue socks. No bag for me, but who needed one?

Mama wasn't left out. Edith brought her a pretty hat, and some beautiful yardage for a new dress. On the first pretty Sunday, Edith took Elda and I to the Coletrain's house, where Miss Benny had a 'Kodak.' (She made pictures for the settlement for a dime each.) We sure made a pretty picture.

Come May meeting, we three girls and mother stepped out in style. This was one time we weren't outdressed by many people. It felt good. It didn't matter that Elda and I wore the same outfit to all three churches, for May meetings. We were dressed fit to kill.

Edith, Elda, & Floe Ellen

Chapter 49
The Chicken Business
1936

This year a new angle for making money came upon the horizon. Juno Pruitt had built a hothouse for raising chickens. Seeing it first hand inspired us to follow suit. Already, Hall county was mopping up in this new industry. It was a great idea, but how to break into it was something else. First, there would have to be the house, then the brooders, feeders, and drinkers.

Elda and Edith discussed this with Daddy, hoping he would volunteer to build the house, but no cigar. Mama suggested building a house of logs. Daddy said if we did, he would furnish the lumber for the decking, window casing, and the door. Mama already had a hundred dollars of Everett's money saved that he was sending home. He said for her to let Edith and Elda have it on a loan. So that would take care of the roof, and the equipment needed. They could get the chickens and the feed furnished until the chickens were sold.

Now to build the house. We cut, skinned, and snaked the logs as soon as the crops were laid by. We then notched and laid them. Then, while the roof was being put on, we began the chore of daubing the cracks. In the side of the nearby red-clay roadbank, we dug out and began to pour water into the hole by the buckets-full. We would scrape the sides and the bottom until the mud was of the right consistancy. Then, bucket by bucket, we hauled on the wheelbarrow, until the last crack was chinked. When the two little win-

Scrap Cotton

dows for ventilation were in and the big opening on the south side was covered in a waxed material, we were ready for the brooders and the nice smelling shavings.

Once the six hundred baby chicks arrived, it was an enjoyable place to spend time. But as the weeks passed, and the chicks grew, the smell became more and more offensive, until one had to summon up a lot of will power just to go in to attend the chores. About fourteen weeks later, Edith and Elda took a profit of about ninety dollars. They were in business, and we all marvelled at the money that could be made with so few hours work each day.

After the first bunch was raised, Edith went back to Griffin. Mama and I took her place. By the time we had raised a couple of bunches, Everett's money was paid back, and we had a nice profit left over. Come spring, though, Daddy said we didn't have time to raise chickens and make a crop, too. So it became a part-time business.

Chapter 50
The Revivals
1936

Revival meeting time was a time of renown. It meant three to four weeks of meetings, day and night. For the young people, it was a time of courtship. A time for boy to meet girl, or most often, a chance to take a second look at the one met last year. People came from near and far for revivals. Different church groups overlapping other church groups. For the older or more fervent Christians, it was a chance to get spiritually revived, and to see people get saved. After all, that was the primary purpose. It was a time of singing, praying, shouting, and some of the very best preaching ever heard.

There sure wasn't any air conditioning in those days, and the windows just weren't adequate to supply the fresh cool air needed. Not even with the employment of the fans furnished by funeral homes and other business. The congregation suffered, but the poor preacherman routinely, progressively perspired to the point of his clothes getting dripping wet.

The poor sinner, or the lost as they were known, were the focal point of it all. Some didn't appear to care that their souls were in danger, and would scoot out as soon as the 'altar call' was given, or else, stand as if defiant. While concerned parents and friends pleaded and prayed, they would relent and come seeking salvation.

There were those who would fall in the altar night after night, meeting after meeting, and some, year after year, crying out to the Lord to be

Scrap Cotton

saved. It seemed these just wouldn't repent, or let go of their sins. Maybe they just couldn't believe that Christ would abundantly pardon. Nothing was sadder than the closing of the last revival of the summer on Saturday night with souls still whimpering on the mourner's bench. Of course they could still make their peace at home, or in the woods; but there would be no revival at the church until next year.

It sounds like a hard way to get saved. But having wept their way to a saving knowledge of Jesus Christ was a way of knowing for sure they were saved. When the last sin was confessed and forgiven, the joy that filled their soul was overwhelming. Almost without exception, there was shouting by the convert, and those who had so feverently prayed for the recipient.

There must have been others like me who patiently, or impatiently, waited for their twelfth birthday, so they could get saved. (Small children, didn't need saving; they were safe as children.) But, when you got about twelve years old, you were eyed as a candidate for the altar. And I'm sure prayer went up in your behalf to be saved. As for me, I was anxious. I sure didn't want to die and go to Hell. The year that I was eleven, this terrible feeling (for the need of a Savior) fell on me one night and I secretly began to pray that I'd be saved.

At the first week of revival at the first church to hold the meeting the next year, I examined myself for the urge to go up. It didn't come until Friday night. The first song they sung, while we were still milling about in the yard, was "Who Is That Knocking?". I knew my time had come. The sermon, "Why halt ye between two opinions?",

The Revivals

fueled my intentions. Then, "O' Why Not Tonight", the song of invitation, and I was on my way to the mourner's bench. I was burdened. I was scared. And I was weeping. I had to have Jesus. Some lady, Mrs. Laura Martin I believe, was kind enough to slip me a handkerchief, which I needed badly.

Soon after I began to pray, I lost contact with my surroundings. It seemed I found myself in dense darkness, never mind there were bright lights in the church. It seemed to me I'd perish in the darkness. Then I could see light. In the distance, I could see light. I began, as it seemed, to crawl toward the light. It got brighter as I drew closer, then I was there. I began to look up. I was prostrate before this towering figure of white light. As I was able to look more directly up, I saw his arms outstretched. I looked harder; I wanted to see his face; but the light blinded my view. Then it all began to dissipate.

I was suddenly aware of my surroundings, but had no desire, yet, to communicate. I sat there calm and peaceful. I was quiet. Edith asked me, "Is everything alright?" I wanted to say, "Yes, yes," but I didn't. I hadn't shouted, and had had no urge to do so. At her persistance, though, I said, "I saw Jesus, but I couldn't see his face." Someone consoled me, "Maybe next time." I was through praying, so I got up and went back to my seat.

Poor Mama couldn't be there that night; she wasn't able at all, so Elda had stayed home with her. I know Edith told Mama that I had been to the altar. But Mama didn't want to embarrass me, so she said nothing. Next day, Daddy took us back. There was no preaching that day, just a

Scrap Cotton

series of testimonies, very spiritual in content. I could hardly sit in my seat. I wanted to testify, too! But I hadn't shouted, therefore I guessed I wasn't qualified, so I kept quiet. The altar call was given, and I didn't go. But a young convert asked if I wasn't going, so I went. But there was no urge to pray; I simply got up again.

That night Mama made herself go, though very sick. I sensed everyone expected me to go up again, so I went, still no urge to pray. Mama asked me if anything had happened. She asked me to look around, "Are the lights brighter?" "Not as bright as the one I saw last night," I told her. At this she began to rejoice. I didn't know what to do, so I did or said nothing.

Next day at the baptizing, I wanted to be baptized more than anything in the world. I just wanted to break and run into the water, but I didn't have a change of clothes with me. During the next week of revival at the next church, I told Mama that I wanted to be baptized on Sunday. And so I was, even though I hadn't shouted. I was now a Christian, and I knew it.

Chapter 51
Dual Purpose

When we first moved to Forsyth, one of the first things we did was to try and find a church. There were three baptist churches relatively close by. The same as at Corinth, they each held Sunday services once a month. Concord on the first Sunday, Mount Tabor on the second, and Zion Hill on the third. Coal Mountain on the fourth, I believe, but it was a little too far to consider a home church. We routinely visited the three closer ones. It took a while for Daddy to decide, but finally he settled on Mount Tabor. We would join ourselves to it.

As far as Sunday School, none of our churches had been designed for it. They consisted of only a large sanctuary. But Mrs. Mattie Jennings, bless her heart, held and taught Sunday School on Sunday evenings at Elmo. This was very close by, and certainly enticing. At the very least, it gave us some place to go. I'll never forget my first pretty Sunday School cards she gave me.

Daddy was not too keen on this. He didn't like the idea of a woman being in charge and teaching. But Mama thought us kids should go, and so we did, enjoying it to the fullest.

We even held revivals at our school on occasion. I remember this Methodist minister who ran a revival. I don't remember his name, but I'll always remember the story he told about this little boy asking his Mama why his Grandpa was so solemn. She told him, "Grandpa has got religion." Then one day, the little boy came running in. He told his mother, "Mama, Mama, our mule's got

Scrap Cotton

religion." Upon which she questioned why he thought so. He announced, "Why Mama, he stands around with his head down all the time." Everybody laughed. It seemed a little irreverent, but I thought the preacher had made a good point, when he added that you didn't have to be sad to be a Christian.

My Mama had a most pleasant personality. She sang and smiled a lot. She seemed to be happy, even when I couldn't see anything she had to be happy about. She was not a sad Christian, for sure!

Chapter 52
Real Cotton Mattresses

With F.D.R. at the helm of the nation, local government now fell into line. There was a surplus of cotton already grown. Therefore, the farmer was being compensated not to continue to add to the stockpiling. At the same time, government was finding ways to utilize as much of it as was possible. One way that was found not only used some of the cotton, but indulged the farmer as well.

There was this program instituted, whereby one could obtain a cotton mattress simply by paying $1.50 for the ticking and cords used to tuft the mattresses. The cotton filling was free. Two members from each family worked with other recipients for a day making the mattresses.

About two dozen of us were notified as to where and when to meet. A couple of supervisors were on hand to instruct us in the cutting out and stitching of our mattresses. They also showed us how to do the whipping, fluffing, and spreading of the cotton, and finally the tufting of the mattress. At the end of the day, each two people proudly carried their mattress home, where ours would replace a straw tick.

Elda and I were the laborers for our mattress, and consequently, got it for our bed. We went back a few weeks later, to repeat for our second mattress that we were entitled to. Daddy and Mama got this one. They already had springs on their bed. Now with a cotton Mattress, and feather tick, they had a really good bed.

Chapter 53
A Cowgirl, Maybe
1936

The evening time was a time of togetherness for our family, the chores done for the day. In the winter time we gathered around the fire for, say, a couple of hours. This time was usually spent listening to Daddy reveal his plans and maneuvers to make more money, pay off his debts, and put us on easy street. These talks, once heartening, were wearing away to empty promises. Everytime Daddy got more money, he simply reinvested in more land. We just never seemed to get there.

Then there were the evenings when he took out his old fiddle and began to play: "Sally Gooden", "Turkey in the Straw", "Alabama Gal", "Leather Britches", on and on. He played pretty good. But after a while, the drone of the fiddle got us all sleepy. At times, it appeared he had played himself to sleep.

In the summertime Edith would go to the old organ in the front room and begin to play. Elda and I would gather around where we would sing gospel songs. Mama and Daddy would sometimes come in to listen. At other times, we would play Everett's big graphanola, which he had left with us along with his collection of records. He had a good selection: some by the Carter family including "Sweet Fern Wilewood Flower" and "Foggy Mountain Top", and some by Jimmy Rogers like "Way out on the Mountain" and "T.B. Blues", and more I can't recall. He even had some negro

A Cowgirl, Maybe

spirituals, and a couple of comedies by the Two Black Crows.

Then came the era of my guitar. I had scraped together $4.98, enough to buy Sears & Roebuck's best guitar. It came with a chord book and instructions. It didn't take long to learn to play the songs contained therein. After this, I disregarded the book, and began to sing and play on my own, using the chords I had learned. Soon Elda had bought herself a mandoline. We both learned enough chords on it, so as to play together. My choice was to play and sing country and western songs, completely releasing the feelings within me.

At this stage of things, I had concluded that I would never be married. Becoming a cowgirl, dominated my thoughts. It wasn't hard to invision myself riding the open range with the vast sky overhead, and the wind in my face, while I galloped a beautiful mount. Smelling the sagebrush, and the cactus in bloom was a little harder to imagine, having never experienced them. But this I knew, riding horseback gave me the greatest feeling of freedom I had ever known.

Chapter 54
Ole Kate and Ole Jim

R.W. and I used to push Daddy's mules to the limit, every chance we got. Putting them through every imaginable maneuver. Racing them, jumping ditches, or making them slide down road banks so steep we had to fight to keep from sliding down over their heads. (I actually cringed in my seat! I again took note of my surroundings, Atlanta couldn't be far ahead.) "What if they had broken a leg, or something?" What would have been our fate? Whew! I guess, we just quit thinking once we were astride our mounts.

There was this time that Daddy let me and R.W. saddle up the mules and go to Julius Pruitt's store, where we were to purchase a few things. On the way over, R.W. had us pull off the road. He dismounted and went behind some bushes from where he brought out a toesack with a dozen or more liquor bottles in it. Obviously, he had been picking them up for a long time.

After we made our purchase at the store, we put the mules in a gallop. We turned toward Barretsville, where he sold the bottles at three cents each. Then we made our own purchase. He bought us a can of Hi Plane and a can of Half-n-half tobacco. We got free cigarette leaves with the tobacco. But he had money left, so he bought a five cent book of OCB leaves. After all, we would be buying sacks of Bull Durham, or Duke's Mixture later on. They only cost a nickle a bag, but you never got enough free leaves to last as long as the tobacco did.

Ole Kate and Ole Jim

With our smoking material intact, we lit up and got ready for the gallop back to our road home. It was necessary to run our mules, so as to make up for the lost time. They could cool the last mile home, so they wouldn't be sweaty when we got there. R.W. said the magic word, RACE!

I had Ole Jim, and he had Ole Kate, and she could outrun anything. So I insisted on a good headstart. [Old Jim had runaway in the past with Everett, (a couple of times).] I had boasted that I hoped he would run away sometime with me; I knew just what I would do. This day Ole Jim did run away with me, and I did just what I had always said I would do. I thought he was running unusually hard, but I kept expecting R.W. to catch up. He couldn't. Ole Kate was flattened out like a flying squirrel, but she couldn't catch us.

R.W. yelled, "He's running away, Floe Ellen!"

"Let him run," I yelled.

I gave him the hickory. Everytime he hit the ground, I hit him. He ran until he grunted each time he hit the ground. We let them run until we were within about a half mile of home. Then I pulled up the rein, and said, "Whoa, Jim." He seemed glad to stop. Then, and only then, he let Ole Kate catch up.

R.W. breathed a sigh of relief. He had been scared stiff. He had expected Ole Jim to start bucking, in which case I would have been thrown off. But he didn't, and I could not have had a bigger thrill. Kids sometimes are just plain dumb, I guess.

Both our mounts were sweaty, and breathing hard when we got home. But this was easy to explain, in that Ole Jim had run away; and R.W., on Ole Kate, had just been trying to keep up.

Chapter 55
Squirrel Dumplings

As a child growing up, I liked riding mules, climbing trees, and hunting. In fact, I guess I was just a 'tom-boy'. Elda was five years older than me, therefore we didn't have a lot in common back then. While the age spread between R.W. and Everett was eight years, R.W. was just three years my senior. Consequently, R.W. and I were more comfortable doing things with each other than with our older siblings.

We built and put out rabbit boxes. R.W. set steel traps, and I'd help him tend them. We actually started hunting together by the time I was ten or eleven, with guns, no less. R.W. would carry the twelve guage shotgun, while I carried Everett's twenty-two rifle. We hunted rabbits and squirrels mostly.

The only rabbits I ever killed were in their beds. But I shot a lot of squirrels out of the trees. This is what I enjoyed the most, because Mama was always so pleased when we brought home squirrels.

We could sit on our front porch and hear the squirrels barking on the hill across the 'big ditch' from us. Sometimes Mama would say to me, "Floe Ellen, I sure would like some squirrel dumplings." That was all the prodding I needed. I would get the rifle and be off. All I had to do was position myself under the hickory nut trees and wait real quiet and motionless until the squirrels would start back moving around. Then I'd wait for one to pose for me, one 'ping', and I had a

Squirrel Dumplings

squirrel for Mama. I would get a couple more, then proudly take them home to her.

Then came the part I didn't like, helping Mama skin and dress them. But soon the squirrels were boiling in the pot, properly seasoned. Once the squirrel meat was tender, Mama would add the milk and her 'special recipe' dumplings! This made a great dish for everyone to enjoy, but Mama really relished it. Though I had a hard time stomaching wild meat, I just loved to please my Mama. So I'd eat some too.

Chapter 56
Here Comes the Bride
1937

The first year that Edith went to Griffin, she got herself a boyfriend that she was real serious about. A city fellow, no less, and, from his picture, looked the part. For some reason or the other, Daddy never approved of any boy we dated. He always knew something derogatory against them. In this case, he just didn't know him at all. I guess that was the problem. "He was probably a big, upity-up, no-good, something. Edith should forget him." When she came home in the spring, they continued to keep in touch by mail. Eventually though, he must have found someone else, for the letters stopped.

Edith stayed home next year; Esther had a maid, and Edith was needed at home. But the next fall, she went back. She met and fell in love with another guy, and it sounded as if they would surely be married. When Daddy pushed her to come back home, this guy gave her an ultimatum: Stay and marry him, or forget him. She came home, but very torn up inside.

By August meeting she had caught the eye of a local boy. By the next spring, they were getting married. Daddy didn't think too much of it, but Mama reminded him that Edith was almost twenty-two years old. He relented, and gave her twenty-five dollars for her trousseau.

Out came the catalogs! Sears & Roebuck, Mongomery Ward, and National Bellas Hess. Bellas Hess, had a lovely outfit on its cover. This was it! A lovely blue dress with white tatting on the

Here Comes the Bride

big collar, and a strip of see-through down the sleeves. It was priced at $4.98!, but this was for a wedding. So, she ordered it, along with white gloves, a hat, a purse, pretty blue sandals, and real silk stockings with the pretty seams down the backs. She ordered a pretty nightgown, and other unmentionables, blowing the whole wad.

She was so pretty, we got all choked-up just looking at her. When Leon came for her, he was just as striking in his blue suit, and his big blue eyes. Matching perfectly, they were a handsome couple. Elda went with them to the wedding. R.W. and I had to stay home with Mama and Daddy.

I was just thirteen, but I got to grow-up fast now. For Elda was not allowed to go anywhere, unless I went with her. Now that Edith was gone, it was the beginning of Elda and me. We didn't fight anymore, for she treated me as her equal. I liked that.

Chapter 57
Growing Pains
1937

Growing up had been painful for me. From stomach worms coming up to choke me, to pin worms that tried to eat me up on the other end (on a certain time of the moon), actually coming out of me sometimes. I had so many, they could be seen squirming in my stools.

Then there were these headaches I started having when I was eleven. My head hurt so severely I couldn't stand light or any noise at all. I couldn't even stand to talk, much less cry, for this just increased the pain. I could only lie under the cover with my head bound in vinegar and brown paper. This occured every two or three months.

I also had leg pains that I suffered with periodically. Sometimes at night, sometimes coming home from school crying with them. Daddy was sure I needed to wear long stockings to keep my legs warm. Then, as if by an angel sent from heaven, someone told him it was probably caused by the rubber bands I wore to hold my stockings up. Saying, "Rubber caused leg pain." All the pain I had experienced in my legs was worth it when he went and bought me anklets like everyone else wore. I denied any further pain, or maybe it actually went away because of the change, I'll never know.

As if these things were not enough to dread, there were the attacks of "cramp colic" as Daddy called it. My entire abdomen would gripe and hurt until it would wring all the strength out of

Growing Pains

me. Then there was vomitting. Daddy bought a couple of bottles of colic medicine, that only tended to nauseate me. Mama would give me diluted linament, then rub camphor on my belly. She would apply a warm iron, wrapped in a towel. Then there was Daddy's 'sure-fire' cure of Epsom salts, his favorite laxative. He would mix them in warm water and tell me to drink them down. My stomach revulsed at the thought. But Daddy said, "Drink," with authority in his voice, and I would chug-a-lug. The mixture would no sooner hit my stomach than up it gushed. I would heave until I could hardly bear it. "Vomitting will break the cramp," Daddy insisted. After about twenty-four hours of terrible suffering, I would fall asleep, the pain gone.

This went on for about three years, the attacks getting closer and harder. I never heard a doctor's name mentioned. Then there was this attack that started on a Saturday night, and by Sunday night I was vomitting fecal matter out of my mouth. By Monday morning, I was delirious. My mind just came and went. I remember coming to myself lying in the front yard. I think the shock of Mama saying, "Here comes the Doctor," brought me to my senses. This was the first doctor to see me since I was born. Doctor Bramlett came and pushed on my stomach a little, then turned to ask what they had been doing for me. When he had their answer, he fumed. "What have you all been trying to do? Kill her? You've done all the wrong things," he said. (Accenting it all with words you wouldn't use in Sunday school.) "Go by and get some ice to make a compress for her stomach. Then get her to Gainsville as quick-

Scrap Cotton

ly as you can. We've got to get her appendix out before it bursts, if it hasn't already."

Daddy asked how much money he would need. When Dr. Bramlett told him $140, Daddy said he had it. This was for the operation, and the ten days I'd need in the hospital. I remember saying, "I'm not worth $140." Daddy replied that he believed I was. I was scared, very scared.

This was a rare and serious operation, and perhaps I'd never wake up. Getting put to sleep by inhaling ether is not a desirable way, believe me. I thought I was strangling to death. Everything was spinning violently, and the terrible ringing in my ears was blasting the last of my senses away.

I did wake up, but a very miserable wretch. My whole family was there encouraging me, but I just wanted a drink of water, then be left alone to die. It is a wonder I didn't. I was too sore to turn over for days, and they didn't make me. Neither did I set foot on the floor until after I went home. I had this long, ugly incision that had required forteen straggling stitches. An appendectomy was quite a feat in those days, but it had to be worth it, not to have to dread another attack.

Though I don't think the two were associated, my headaches quit coming, too, about this time. The worm problem had already ceased, as well as my leg pain. I guess they had just been childhood disorders. As Mama had said, I had outgrown them, but it had taken some doing.

Chapter 58
Poetry in Motion
1937

Growing up in the country sure had its good and abiding points. It was challenging, as well as fascinating to till the soil. Whether it was watching the first slicing of the soil in preparation for the seed, or seeing the geometrical patterns coming into being as the furrows or rows went in, or at each and every working of the plants, until the final harvest was finished. I know of no field of endeavor with a more visible reward for your labor than working with the soil.

With all the toil and sweat, there is also that blessed moment of rest, cooling from the sun at the end of each row. There were usually green trees with an inviting shade where one could look back and admire their accomplishments, and anticipate the job ahead. It was in these moments I liked to daydream. (In fact, we were reminded more than once we were resting too long.) My favorite place was beside a gurgling, cooling stream. My most favorite spot was where we forded the creek to our lower bottoms. It was here, a poem began to form in my mind, while I daydreamed. And when I went home, I put it down on paper. I wrote:

"Life"
I sat one day by a bubbling brook,
    while a cool breeze tossed my hair.
It was there I tried to concentrate
    on life, I felt unfair.

Scrap Cotton

> I viewed a bubble, while far away,
>   just a tiny thing at first.
> As it drew near, my nerves grew tense,
>   afraid that it would burst.
> For somehow, I imagined it to be
>   my very life, I seen.
> Could it be, it could survive
>   the roughness of the stream?
> I scanned again, the bubbling brook,
>   many bubbles were in view.
> Some seemed large, and old, and tough,
>   while others seemed small and new.
> Some could take the roughest spots,
>   and still come out OK.
> While others burst at the slighest jolt,
>   and some just faded away.
> There was this roughest, toughest spot
>   they all had to go down.
> Where they found calm waters
>   in which to float around.
> And so it is, the same with life,
>   always struggling to its goal.
> Some go on while others stop,
>   and give up life and soul.
> So after all, life's fair enough
>   just a race we must not slack.
> For once a soul has passed this way,
>   it never can come back.

I wrote this poem at thirteen. Not for publicity, not for posterity, I wrote this poem for me. I had taken a long look at my soul, and talked with the same.

Poetry in Motion

I had written my first poem the year before, and sent it to the local newspaper. It came out in the next week's paper. It made me feel real good, seeing my poem in print. But not one soul, except my family, mentioned seeing it. My first poem was written in an entirely different setting.

The day had been a dismal and rainy Sunday. I think it must have been my first encounter with boredom. R.W. was gone off, and Elda was sleeping. I didn't have my guitar yet, so I couldn't sing or play, as I would have later. I liked to draw, so I got myself some paper and a pencil, and went out and got in our ole '28 Chevrolet Sedan. I sketched a few profiles, and tried to draw a new car or two, but this just didn't get it.

I was concerned with my future, and I didn't see any-way I wanted to go. Growing up, and marrying a farmer just didn't appeal to me. I wanted something different, and Mama would never consent to us girls going away to public works. Just working for Esther, as Edith had for three dollars a week, wouldn't get it either. Besides, we would always have to come home to make a crop in the spring. There had to be a way! There had to be something better! So I wrote:

"We Can Build a Future"

Some of us have our memories,
    on which we can rely.
When gloom over takes us
    and clouds vale the sky.
But what if we have lived
    a life that's hard to face.
Then our many memories
    can not our grief erase.

Scrap Cotton

"There's just no rhyme or reason,"
   some people sometimes say.
My life is O' so empty,
   just drags from day to day.
But yes, life is over-flowing,
   though it may be with grief.
If there is still a future,
   then there can still be peace.
So why not leave behind us,
   the old life we have lived.
And start today to builing,
   the future we should build.
For our past we can not bring back,
   nor our wrongs undo.
But we can build a future,
   and live in it too.

Maybe, I wouldn't make a career of writing poetry. But I could say things in rhyme that gave me more expression than I could express in any other way.

Floe Ellen

Chapter 59
Lily White

In the settlement where we lived, it was not uncommon for the women folk to go to the field to hoe or to pick cotton. These were accepted jobs for women. But one thing was for sure; you weren't suppose to look like it on Sunday. You were to be as white as city folk, and we were.

With the sun bearing down on you all day long in the fields, you had to protect yourself. We wore 'bonnets' or wide brimmed straw hats. (Hats were my choice.) We wore overalls to protect our legs, long sleeved shirts to shield our arms, 'neck rags' around our necks, and gloves on our hands. One could buy gloves for ten or fifteen cents, but most often we wore men's old socks on our hands. The socks that were uniform for men were loose knit ones. These stretched easily, enabling the thumb to expand out and around your hoe handle. This protected from the sun, and helped protect against corns. It helped, but it didn't completely eliminate them.

For all intent and purposes, you 'worked' but you weren't supposed to show it. Some women folk in our community, it appeared, didn't have to work. Maybe they did work in the back fields off the big road, but who could tell? It seemed that just about anytime you passed their house, you could see them sitting on the front porch in their starched and ironed dresses.

One thing I know for sure, older women, like Mama, didn't go to the field. They had enough to keep them busy keeping the house clean, preparing the meals, washing, ironing, sewing, canning,

Scrap Cotton

and maybe working in the garden. But Daddy expected us all to do "field time". Never-the- less, when we were bathed and dressed for Sunday, we were still lily white, or at least as white as anybody else.

Chapter 60
Elmo Burned
1937

There had been much discussion on school consolidaton. The school board, it seemed, wanted to close our small school, and bus us kids to Matt. My Daddy, and some of the other older, if not wiser, heads gave an emphatic, "NO!" "Too much meanness over there for our kids to encounter," they said. They wanted us to stay and finish the eighth grade at Elmo.

While the tug of minds was still going on, our school house burned one night. Arson was foremost in everyone's mind. This was nothing but a ploy to force us to consolidate. Not so! The men of the community banned together to build anew. All contributing to the cause in labor and materials. (Daddy donated lumber, I know.) In hardly any time, a new school was built, with an updated light consideration. All of the windows were on one side, with us sitting with our backs to the windows; the light would shine over our shoulders and onto the blackboard.

We had a better, but smaller, schoolhouse now. It had but one room, and only went throught the seventh grade. We won after all!!?!?

It was here I would complete my formal education, finishing the seventh grade the first year, but going back part-time for two more years. Partly to make Mama and Daddy happy by staying in school, but mostly to keep me happy by not staying home. I much preferred being with other children, playing ball, and being the "big one" in school. The smaller children looked up to

Scrap Cotton

me as if I were a grown-up. Besides, I did increase my learning somewhat.!

Chapter 61
A Growing Family Tree
1938

When Edith and Leon married, they moved in with Leon's mother and father for the first year, helping them make a crop. By the next year, they had rented a place where they share cropped. Leon had his own mule, the same one he had ridden to come court Edith. Mr. Claude Bailey, his father, owned a buggie they could always borrow. That was how Leon and Edith got around.

By the end of the year, LaRue, their oldest child, was born. She was very special to all of us, in that she was our only niece or grandchild living close by. I call it 'close by', actually they lived about six miles away. But it wasn't too far to walk. I walked it many times. I would go spend Saturday night with them every chance I got.

Edith was always very special to me. Now that she was married, and had a baby too, it was a real treat to get to go to her house. She could bake the best biscuits, fry the best fat back, and make the best water gravy I ever ate. (Nobody could make 'milk gravy' better than Mama though.)

Another thing that made going to Edith's and Leon's special was they had a deck of Rook Cards. They taught me how to play Rook. Mama and Daddy wouldn't allow a deck of cards in our house. So, it was not only challenging to play Rook, it was daring as well. It seemed Daddy and Mama were just too peculiar, this was fun.

Then too, there was the thrill of getting to ride in the buggie. A buggie ride was unique to me. If I

Scrap Cotton

had walked up there on Saturday, they would bundle up LaRue, and we would all crowd into the buggy. They would drive me home on Sunday. Where we would eat a special dinner Mama would prepare. It was real cozy, having a married sister, and her family to go visit, and to have them come to visit us. This gave us something else to look forward to, and God knows we needed a diversion.

Edith & Leon Bailey

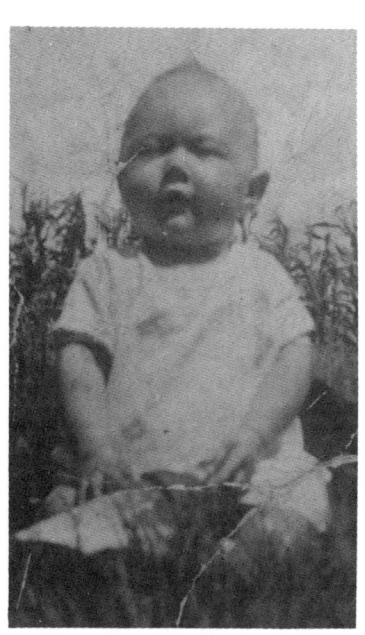

La Rue Bailey

Chapter 62
The Open Door

Through-out the architectural ages, doors have played such an important role in our lives, making a statement for those who design them as well as for those who dwell behind them. In my time and area, there were some more noteworthy doors, but most were of necessity.

Our doors were opened for ventilation or closed for warmth. In the summer, they were never closed, even at night. The visitors never knocked, instead they stood outside and shouted, "Hello!" and waited until someone came to the door. (The dog saw to that.) Or if they came by car, they honked until someone came to invite them in. The burglars or robbers just never came, while the flies and other insects came and went at will. (Thank Heavens, we just didn't have many mosquitoes.) Oh, most folks had screens. We had one on the kitchen door, but for a lot of people, there were none. If they had had screens, the cracks would have let the flies in anyway. Therefore, there was the necessity of the 'fly drives'.

When we had our breakfast, or our supper at night, the flies were sluggish or asleep on the ceiling. At dinner, it was a different story, though. It was almost like a swarm of bees in the big kitchen, therefore the fly drive was a necessary ritual. Always, a couple of peachtree limbs heavy with leaves, were brought in before dinner was ever put on the table. Then everyone got a towel or a piece of news paper. (Mama always used her apron.) First we would shoo the flies from the

Scrap Cotton

back corners. Then, having them shoo'd to the center of the room, we all began to wave our "shoo-ers" anxiously toward the door where the flies all rushed out. This was repeated two or three times until there were no more than a smattering of flies left. Then the screen door was closed. The peach-tree limbs kept the straglers waved away from the table while we ate. Before the flies could find their way around and back into the house, our dinner would be finished. When, say, the preacher would come home with us during revival, or other company, that necessitated the white cloth on the table, the 'fly drives' started earlier and were repeated until hardly one of the little varments could be found.

When the meal was finished, what food was left was placed in the bottom of the cupboard. Even though there was a crack at the top of the door, it still was dark inside. Therefore the flies did not invade. The food was neatly tucked with a guano sack towel just in case. If a fly was found in the food, we just wouldn't eat it.

There were locks on all of the outside doors, but frankly, I don't remember ever seeing the key for them. We did have, and used, a pull-string latch on the kitchen door. Plus, there were whittled twirly buttons on most of the doors. These, as I remember, were mostly used in case of high winds, so as to keep the door from blowing open.

The door said, "Welcome, friend."
The dog said, "Halt, stranger."
The shot-gun said, "Thief or robber, beware."

Chapter 63
The Summer Death Hovered
1938

The fourth of July was fondly thought of as 'laying-by' time. Therefore, a celebration, if no other way than by pitching our hoes in the air with a whoop and a shout. Sometimes it meant ice-cold lemonade for the entire community, made in a tub, and served up with the family dipper.

For several years we had been going to Tommy Turner's for a 'Turner' celebration. There were always tables and tables of food, and perhaps two or three tubs of lemonade. (He was a Turner, and we were Turner's, but of very distant, if any, kin.) Being the congenial fellow that he was, he invited us to attend. With him it was, in reality, the "more the merrier". But this year, we chose the Stubblefield invitation. It was complete with a baseball game, played in a cow pasture, for real. (With all the cow dropping obstacles to look out for.)

This, however, was one of the years we had not finished all the hoeing Daddy wanted done. But we got to go to celebrate anyway, going back to the field later to finish up. We had come in for dinner, and Elda and I were swinging on the front porch, before returning to the field. I had on a pair of repaired shoes, which I had cut the top of the toe out of, so the dirt would sift through and not pack up inside. There was a tack in the sole that Mama had failed to brad, because it was at the very tip of the then closed toe. This caught Elda in the heel, and it bled profusely for a small

Scrap Cotton

puncture. Mama had her soak it in kerosene, and it was soon forgotten about.

A couple of weeks later, she said it felt as if a bee had stung her in the bend of the knee, but there was no sign. From that, the pain persisted. Then the leg began to swell, and turn red in back. A few days later, her pain was so intense, Daddy took her to see Doctor Marcus Mashburn in Cumming. He ordered her leg elevated, and hot poltices applied. Then he went away for a few days. When her condition worsened with a high fever, Daddy went and got Dr. R.H. Bramblett. He gave her some medicine. But in a couple of days, with her becoming delirious, Daddy went for Dr. Brablett again. This time, without anything for pain, while we held her on the bed, he attempted to lance it, getting only blood. "She is dangerously ill," he told us. So he sent her to Hall county hospital. By the time we got her there, her fingernails and toenails had already turned purple, and her eyes were dark and sunken.

Elda & Floe Ellen

Once in the hospital, they began to medicate her with hands full of big pills, which we later learned were sulfa drugs. She hovered between life and death for about five days. Two weeks later, when she was allowed to come home, she looked like a corpse, so pale and skinny. Her leg had finally been lanced. It looked as if all the muscle had drained out of the back of

The Summer Death Hovered

her leg. Where the calf had been, was now fallen in. But she was alive!

I had almost lost my sister. This would have been unbearable for me. It was all because of me and that stupid tack. How thankful I was that sulfa drugs had become available, and just in time to save my 'sis'.

Chapter 64

The 'Possum Hunt

It had always been our lot to have good dogs. They were well trained to hunt rabbits and squirrels by day, and 'possums and 'coons by night. Elda, R.W., and I did a lot of possum hunting. Hides brought a dollar and half each. R.W. took care of killing the possums. I helped with the skinning. Next he stretched and nailed the hides to the side of the barn to tan.

One hunt, I remember, we hadn't planned. We just heard the dogs treed over the hill in the pasture where there were persimmon trees. We grabbed our toesack, the axe, and the lantern. We had no problem getting the possum out of the tree, except he relieved himself right on the top of R.W.'s head. Elda laughed so hard, she rolled on the ground. Luckily, we were real close to the branch, so R.W. washed it out as best he could.

Meanwhile, the dogs treed again. We put our possum in the sack, and Elda threw it over her back. While we were going to get the second one, the possum relieved himself again. Needless to say, it went right through the toesack. Now it was our turn to laugh at her, while she moaned and gagged. Once the second one was bagged, it was on to home, and baths for both of them, even though it wasn't Saturday night.

Then there was the time we had a community hunt with about a dozen of us young folks going. It was a sheer delight to listen to the dogs run. First hot on the trail, then maybe the trail lost, or run cold. Then the hot trail picked up again. We knew exactly what was happening by the dog's

The 'Possum Hunt

bark. Then would come the treed bark! We would rush to the scene, ready to shake the possum out or cut down the tree.

We had bagged about six, when we decided it was time to start for home. The only problem being, no-one could agree on exactly which way to go. While we pondered that question, the dogs caught scent of another, and treed again. Once we had him, we started our uncertain path out of the woods. Coming to a branch with high banks, we searched until we found this sandbar on which to jump down.

When it came my turn, I jumped. When I landed, I turned my ankle and fell prostrate. I found I could in no wise walk, and that was that! I would have to be carried. R.W. and another boy, endeavored, making a 'pack-saddle', (holding their own wrist with one hand, while holding the other's wrist with their other hand). It didn't work. I was too heavy, being about fourteen years old. Finally, they just took turns carrying me on their back.

It was about two in the morning when we finally found our way home. As usual, Mama was sitting on the front porch waiting. But she wasn't too worried this time, since she knew there were so many of us. But she knew something had happened, none the less. My swollen foot got the usual vinegar poltice, and I was on crutches for a few days.

The most memorable hunt of all came when Elda, R.W. and I followed Ole Sherman, the best hunting dog we ever owned, into some dense and strange territory down on the creek. It was late, and we had had no results. Some nights, the possums were just not out on the prowl. Sherman

Scrap Cotton

was finally hot on a trail, when suddenly his bark changed to a startled, and somewhat quizzical tone.

He wasn't running a possum anymore. Neither was he doing a 'no-no' by jumping and running a rabbit. He was frightened, and was coming back to us. Ole Sherman had never done this before. R.W., who never showed fright, said, "Something is chasing him." The red nosed briars were so thick here, it was quite difficult to move, but move we did, in the direction of home. Ole Sherman was soon with us, right under our feet, but still barking as if there was something in the shadows.

We were scared, real scared. But Daddy and Mama had always said, "Don't run from a wild animal. It will pursue. Just walk fast, and keep a light." Keep a light? Our lantern was beginning to dim. We were soon out of the dense undergrowth, Thank God, but our lantern was running out of oil. We had forgotten to fill it before we left. Whatever was out there, number one, IT was following us. Number two, Ole Sherman was afraid of it. We had never seen him afraid of anything before. He would tangle with a raccoon and hang in there for the kill. He could whip any dog that would entangle him.

This thing followed us to our pasture. The flame of our lantern was feeding on nothing more than the wick when we hit the clearing. Mama must have been praying for our safety, for, whatever it was that had been stalking us didn't follow onto the open ground. Now Sherman took on more valour, and stayed at the edge of the woods barking, until we were within the lights of home, where he joined us. After that, I preferred

The 'Possum Hunt

rabbit and squirrel hunting in the broad light of day.

Chapter 65
Surprise! Surprise!
1939

Other than Mama baking a cake, birthdays got very little attention. But this year Mama and we girls decided to give R.W. a surprise birthday dinner. We girls got out and invited all the neighbors the week before.

R.W.'s birthday fell on Saturday, and we let it go by practically unnoticed. Saturday night, R.W. went off; he was eighteen years old now. Mama and we girls were up until late cooking, yet R.W. had not come home Mama was getting worried.

We girls went to bed about eleven o'clock. Mama did, too, but I doubt she got much sleep. We were up early next morning to further prepare for the dinner. Daddy didn't know it, but R.W. still wasn't home. Mama was crazy with worry. We girls were worried too, but dared not admit it.

Finally, Daddy said, "Get R.W. out of that bed!" I took it on myself to go upstairs in pretense of awakening him, coming back down to announce he wasn't home. After all, Daddy would have to know sooner or later. Needless to say, this infuriated him.

What on earth were we to do? The neighbors would soon be coming in to celebrate R.W.'s birthday, and R.W. not here! We were all frantic with worry. R.W., nor any other one of us, had ever been out all night before.

It was almost ten o'clock when he came in. Obviously without any sleep. The occasion saved the day for him. There wasn't time to question or

Surprise! Surprise!

fuss. He was, instead, promptly instructed, "Get your Sunday clothes on. We are having company." He was still dressing when the neighbors started coming in, each bringing food as well.

R.W. was surprised alright, but he surprised us first. We'll never know just how he had celebrated his eighteenth birthday, but he sure knew how to live dangerously. Daring to stay out all night without permission, even if he was eighteen.

R.W.'s 18th Birthday

Chapter 66
A Bachelor Ties the Knot
1939

Everett was an ambitious young man. He seemed to always be on the top of the pile. After he had tried his hand at the cotton mill, he decided to join the CCC's. He sent twenty-five dollars per month home to save, and kept only five dollars for spending money. He didn't drink or waste his money. When he came out, he worked for different men at various jobs. He drove a nice car and was always well dressed. Yet he hadn't gotten married. When Mama broached the subject to him, he told her that he'd marry one day, but not until he had something to offer a woman.

Everett & Lorene

At last, when he was twenty-six, he brought Lorene Castleberry home one Sunday to announce this was his bride-to-be. She was a lovely young girl of sixteen, a little young, maybe. But she was mature enough to keep an imaculate house that Everett had furnished with nice new furniture, when they married.

It made us all very proud to see how well they were doing. Everett now had a job with the county earning seventeen dollars per week. A couple of years later they had their first little girl. They

A Bachelor Ties the Knot

named her Janice. She was as cute as a button. We didn't get to see much of them, though, since they lived in Jasper.

It thrilled us all, the day they brought Janice to see us when she was seven months old. It was unreal to see her come walking across the floor. Yes, Everett was happily married, at last.

Chapter 67
Let There Be Light
1939

It was a very dim world that we lived in, but we were not aware of it. To me, it looked bright and inviting to be finishing up the nightly chores, and see the oil lamp sitting on the table. It told a story all its own. It meant Mama was out of the cookroom, and supper was on the table. Only one thing could add to its beauty, and that was in winter when the added flickering of a fire in the fireplace enhanced the scene.

For the most part, night meant the needlework was put away. Mama said her eyes were just too dim to see at night. Therefore, we were excused as well. During school days we were not just idle at night. When school was in, it meant the books after supper, and lots of studying to be done by lantern light or fire light.

We usually had two kerosene lamps, and the lantern. We didn't see the need of a lamp for every room, when it was so easy to carry one from room to room. As cheap as kerosene was, we still didn't burn an extra lamp, unless it was absolutely necessary. One lamp in a room, with a good clean globe, was a bright light to us. Until we saw an "Aladdin" lamp one of our neighbors bought. Compared to it, our light was indeed dim, but we knew we would never own one of those.

Then came the news, electricity was coming to our community. It would be available to anyone subscribing to it. Daddy talked about it, joking as it were, "If we get electricity, the piece of meat we've been hanging over the table won't give us a

Let There Be Light

shadow to sop any longer." He just wouldn't get serious. Mama and we girls fantasized as to what it would be like, and we weren't joking. We hung onto every word Daddy said concerning it, trying to determine his intent.

When the tall creosote poles were put in on the big road in front of our property, we viewed them with awe. We even relished the odor they gave off. They had an odor synonymous with the aroma of town. But when a crew of men arrived at our house with spools of wire, and a box of little white things (which turned out to be light fixtures), we were estatic! We didn't have long to wait after that, until our very own poles were set in place between us and the big road.

Then, LIGHT! I will never forget the day. The bulbs must have been about sixty watts, but light, O' brilliant light! The big catch, (that seemed to come with every good thing), was it cost money to use. A dollar and twenty-five cents per month for fourteen killowats. This was the minimum charge, and we were instructed that it had better not run over. Therefore, these lights were treated under the same order as our oil lamps. They were burned sparingly.

Daddy's joke about the 'meat shadow' fell flat. Our light, brilliant as it was, didn't eliminate the shadows objects cast, after all.

Chapter 68
Convenience at Last
1939

With the power line, of course, came light. But, before the summer was over, Daddy came in with an electric iron. It had a heat control, but we were immediately instructed that it was to be used swiftly, and not too hot, so as not to run up the electric bill. Watts and kilowatts were brand new to our vocabulary, but we learned about them right away. We would stand and watch that wheel go round, and watch cautiously, as the watts built up into kilowatts.

Mama wanted to improve over the control of the iron. We were to use it until it got hot. Then promptly unplug, and iron as much as we could before it got cold, to the point of needing to be plugged in again. I had always been impressed by Mama's intellect; now this didn't impress us at all. But Mama was just cautious and careful of waste.

The iron had surprised and delighted us. But an even bigger and better surprise was in store. Esther's husband, Clarence, was a radio repairman. Clarence had his shop in part of their house, and fixed radios in his spare time. There were few people around who could work on a radio, therefore business was good. Sometimes, someone would be unable to pay their radio out. They just wouldn't come back for it. Therefore, Clarence would have an extra radio now and then.

We had been gone for the day this Sunday. When we came home, a radio was sitting on a

Convenience at Last

table, hooked up, and ready to play. A note was there, explaining it was their gift to us from Clarence and Esther.

Hooray! Hallelujah! We had our own radio. But, it used electricity, and the time alotted for it to play was confined to news broadcasts, and thirty minutes for the "WSB Georgia Jubilee" at dinnertime. Then thirty minutes for the "WSB Barn Dance" on Saturday night. Then maybe, just maybe, thirty more minutes of the "Grand Ole Opry." That was the 'alotted' time, anyway. We discovered "Lorenzo Jones," "Young Widow Brown," "Stella Dallas," and "Backstage Wife" that came on on weekday afternoons. (WSB was the only station we could get.)

We liked them all, but Mama said we would have to weed them out. That all four was too long. We left off "Lorenzo Jones" and "Backstage Wife." When Daddy would be gone, we would get to listen to the other two, but we had to cut out lights, and iron with the sad iron in the wintertime so as to conserve electricity.

It wasn't long before Daddy had a pump put in the well. This was a big improvement. What, with watering the stock, especially when we were raising chickens, it beat the heck out of twisting that old windlass, pulling out a bucket at a time. It sure was nice having all those conveniences.

Chapter 69
Music Appreciation

If and when it looked like we would have a few watts left over on our allowed fourteen killowats, we usually utilized it playing the radio. On this Saturday, as was usual, Daddy was gone off. We seemed to have a few watts to spare. After the twelve o'clock news went off, there didn't seem to be anything on that I wanted to listen to. None- the- less, every so often I would check the programming.

In my persistence, I turned on "Music Appreciation." This sounded promising. I loved music of all kinds, but this was somewhat confusing. It was totally new to me, but I hung in there, determined to learn to 'appreciate' it.

The strands of music were very pretty and harmonious. But I just couldn't pick up on the tune or the timing. Everytime I thought I was beginning to catch on, it all changed. They sounded (to me) as if they might be just warming up. Surely, soon they would strike up a tune and really play something. But for some reason, they just never did, even though I stayed with them through the whole program.

The following Saturdays, I tuned them in again and again, determined to learn to appreciate this music, even though I was convinced by now, it was of a foreign nature. Even the language of the Master of Ceremonies sounded foreign. Symphonic music simply took a lot of getting used to, but I did learn to appreciate it.

Chapter 70
Political Clout

1940 found "Gene" Talmadge again Governor of Georgia for the third time. Still snapping his red gallouses and fighting the unruly lock of hair that hung on his forehead. The people just didn't know when they had had enough of this well educated, yet home spun man.

He seemed to have the unique ability to rally the common man, and at the same time attract a lot of the not-too- common people. When he was first elected in 1933, I can remember everyone climbing aboard his band wagon (Daddy included). He was promising everyone a three dollar tag. This saved the common man five to ten dollars, while at the same time it saved the big corporations thousands of dollars. This evidently elected him.

I never understood why the people rallied around him so. Talmadge fought FDR's New Deal from the start, opposing health and work insurance, especially the NRA's effort to establish the forty-cent- per-hour minimum wage. (It was rumored that he made the statement that 'a man in overalls wasn't worth more than a dollar a day.') Esther and Clarence hated his guts, but Talmadge was Daddy's man. Tensions mounted between them anytime Gene's name was brought up.

When the textile industry struck in 1934, he called out the state troopers to quell the strike agitators. Positioning them on the roofs of mills, armed with tear gas and machine guns, instilling fear into the hearts of the strikers.

Scrap Cotton

When he refused to pay the minimum wage to his highway workers, U.S. funds were cut off. Talmadge simply declared martial law in a restricted area, and put the state to building its own roads.

Despite all the controversy, Gene was elected to another two year term. Still ruling with an iron hand, if his appointees failed to do his bidding, he would simply let them go, and appoint someone who would. Talmadge, being unable to run again, made a futile bid for the senate.

Enter Euritha D. Rivers, promising something much more vital than Talmadge's three dollar tag. He promised "free school books for any student desiring an education". He declared he was in full agreement with FDR's New Deal, and would work harmoniously with him.

Rivers opposed Talmadge's strong hand tactics. It was a two year honeymoon with him. He was elected again in 1938, but there was a sad awakening, when it was realized that he had run the state into terrible debt. Realizing something had to be done, he attempted to have prohibition revoked in an effort to bring in more revenue. Christians and bootleggers joined in the effort to stop this. He tried, in vain, to tap the highway funds. Then, resorting to Talmadge's tactics, he declared martial law to secure the funds he sought.

E.D. Rivers, not being able to run again, bowed out. Talmadge with his famous charisma and help of his old reliable county unit system, was able to fight again. This time it was more focused on the University System, which Talmadge claimed was favoring integration.

He was a fighter, always would be. He undoubtedly was the most colorful governor Georgia

Political Clout

had ever had, or ever would have. His political clout would long be remembered.

Chapter 71
Busy Fingers

When we first moved to Forsyth we were introduced to another handiwork, chenille. Everyone was making chenille bedspreads. One would buy their sheet, unshrunk, then place it over the back side of an already completed spread. Then rub off the design with a snuff box lid, or by using a carbon paper. It was ready for stitching. Making a longer stitch on the top, and a very small stitch on the underside.

When all the stitching was done with a large multiple-ply type thread, the long stitch was clipped and fluffed. Finally the spread was washed, the fabric would shrink on the tufts. Presto! A nice spread, very colorful, and easy to care for.

Chenille spreads, and even embroidered spreads (which had been customary with us), were a far cry from the two counterpanes Mama had from her girlhood. These had really required diligence in making.

Mama gave us a rundown as to how her double-wove counterpanes were made. They grew their own cotton. Sat around the fire at night picking out the seeds. Then it was ready to be combed or carded. Then expertly rolled off the cards into rolls. These rolls were caught on the spindle of the spinning wheel and stretched and spun into threads. Then threaded into the multiple harnessed loom. Next, the shuttle filled with threads shoved through, by a pedal the harnesses were reversed. The thread packed and the shuttle

Busy Fingers

shoved through again and again until a beautiful fabric was complete.

We owned a spinning wheel and cards, (another bonus left with our place when we bought it). Therefore we too spun a lot of thread, but this was used for knitting and crocheting. We also had quilting frames which we used for quilting dozens of quilts. We pieced quilts from numerous patterns that we traded one neighbor with the other. We saved every scrap from our dresses we cut and sewed, as well as ordering 'scrap bundles' from the catalogues. Some of the scraps we saved were hardly more than strings. These we sewed onto our paper patterns. Then we trimmed and pieced the shapes together to make quilt tops, finally pulling off the paper patterns.

The batten for our quilts, we salvaged from our ginned cotton before it was pressed into bales. The back, hardly ever being purchased (except for our finer quilts), was usually feed sacks sewn together. They were then dyed in the washpot, or on occasions dyed by placing it in a hole of red clay and water. But the prettiest of the lot was to dye them in poke-berry juice. Some times we just randomly splashed and sprinkled them. (I guess you could have called it Modern Art.)

Quilting was the most practiced craft. We kept the quilting frames occupied all winter long. Usually they were hung upstairs out of the way. But in order to prevent frost bitten toes, they were brought down and hung in our spacious kitchen. Whereas Mama quilted every spare moment, we girls were a little spasmodic.

I personally preferred embroidering. I embroidered a spread that will, no doubt, be

Scrap Cotton

around a hundred years or more. I did a lot of table runners and doillies, too.

    Mama saw that all seven of us children had a total of six quilts a piece, plus one very special quilt each. Then we girls could have all we were willing to make. I stopped at seven.

Chapter 72
A 'Saxy' Issue

With the coming in of the hot-house chicken industry, came a whole new way to dress. This being the chicken-feed sack dress. An awful lot of people wore them. Those who did not raise chickens could buy the sacks at a dime each. (Each sack contained more than a yard of cloth.) Sewn, starched, and ironed, you had a very pretty dress, a dress for about thirty cents, even if you had to buy the sacks.

These sacks came in multiple floral designs. They were expertly mixed and matched by the distributor, so as to provide at least three or more bags that matched. If, by chance, you received odd patterns, you could always trade with a neighbor.

Already, other feed sacks had been being used to make shirts. In our case, Mama made Daddy's drawers from them. Daddy wore these winter and summer, and wore no other undergarment on his lower extremities. Mama kept a pattern that was made to fit at the waist with a drawstring, thereby being called drawers, I assume. A small band was sewn at the bottom to fit them about the ankles.

The ever usable flour sack was too flimsy for garments, other than maybe bloomers, or a petticoat. Their uses were, none-the-less, numerous. Mama used one for a pastry rolling cloth. They were used for churn covers, for straining milk fresh from the cow, for squeezing juice for jelly, for bandages, or any use where a good soft cloth was needed.

Scrap Cotton

The guano sack, Wow, it was strong. It was thick, and it was rough, but such pretty white pieces of material once it was bleached out. It was used for many things. Sheets for one, you had to just about wear them out before they were really pliant enough for comfort though. They made pretty good towels, though a little stiff. Mama tried making shirts from them, but they were just too stiff, feeling somewhat like a canvas, the menfolk said.

What they were best for was pea threshing sheets, or sheets for emptying and tying up your load of cotton for the day. They were tough enough to make ideal pick-sacks, used for picking cotton or peas. They were ideal, since your pick-sack got dragged on the ground a lot, (a lot of picking was done crawling along on your knees). For peas and the like, the guano sack's close weave kept sharp ends from sticking through and pricking your legs so badly.

Sacks used for these purposes didn't have to have the letters bleached out. But all the white sacks used for personal use had to be treated at length with lye soap and hot potash water. Still, one could sometimes make out the 'R' or another letter from Rosters written on the guano sacks.

Your 'croaker', or 'toesack' as we called them, had their uses too. But they were in and around the barn, containing grain of one sort or another. They made good saddle blankets, and were ideal to spread over and hold the steam in when you were scalding a hog.

At our house we utilized very nearly everthing, being industrious as we were. Hardly anything was ever wasted; it was recycled/reused as long as it would hold together.

Chapter 73
An Uneasy World
1938-1941

Since Roosevelt's taking office, everything seemed financially improved, if not ideal. The economy was still somewhat depressed, but people were eating lots better. More people were working; wages were better; and the farmers were getting a decent price for what they grew.

Hollywood was having a 'hey-day'. Even though we didn't get to see the movies, we did get to read about them in magazines that somehow got bought and circulated through the comminuty. We knew their pictures. Tyrone Power, Mickey Rooney, Spencer Tracy, George Goble, and, of course, Roy Rogers, and Gene Autry, to name a few. But big with me, and evidently everyone else, was Clark Gable. His picture had graced the fronts of our tablets for two or three years, now, replacing the Cherokee rose and the blue horsehead. Shirley Temple had stolen everyone's heart. Jane Withers was a darling. Then there was Carole Lumbard, Bette Davis, Alice Faye, Joan Crawford, and the likes. Reading about their antics and their daring poses shocked me. And for sure, we kept our magazines hid from Mama and Daddy.

There was a world's fair in New York. Here, Germany had set herself apart by staying away. Yet the country, it seemed, was getting giddy again, according to the opinion of many. Just like before the big crash. Yet there was a cloud of gloom over the land. There was too much talk of

Scrap Cotton

war to ignore. With radio now, everyone was getting the news. The uneasiness increased.

Hitler's Germany was swallowing up one little nation after the other. Roosevelt, as calmly as possible, was trying to alert the nation of impending danger. He had already asked for a "Two Ocean Navy," and eight thousand airplanes. The Japanese and the Soviets signed an armistice agreement, so as to ensure Russia would not assist China, in her defense against Japan's effort to overthrow her. Russia and Germany were calling the British and French 'warmongers', while they themselves divided the spoils in Poland. Russia and Germany had signed a non-agression pact with each other, just prior to Germany's attack on Poland. Neither France nor England would ditch their alliance with Poland, so they were the warmongers. Now we were as leery of Russia as we were of Germany.

Americans stood ready to defend America. But no-one seemed willing to get our boys involved, as long as we ourselves were not attacked. Meanwhile, FDR pleaded with Capitol hill to help arm friendly nations. He was aware that Hitler stood in awe of America's vast wealth, and that this mad-man had declared the whole world was his ultimate goal.

By September 1940, congress passed a one year draft, requiring the registration of all men between twenty-one and thirty-five. By October, sixteen-thousand men had registered with the attitude of "Oh, Well. What was one year, if they had to go?" Within the month, the eligible boys began receiving their greetings. Soon, thereafter, their one-year hitch was extended to eighteen months.

An Uneasy World

By 1941, FDR knew he could not step down as he had planned. He felt compelled to seek a third term in office. Preparedness, now, was the watch word. Just before the election, Roosevelt assured the people, "Your boys will not be sent into any foreign wars." But now, by mutual agreement, he was giving Britian everything he could get his hands on. He was mobilizing industry, and arming the country to its teeth.

Optimism was dying. Reality was beginning to dawn. The ominous clouds of war hung heavy.

Chapter 74
Then There Were Two
1941

Though wages were better, Daddy was still managing to keep help for a dollar and a quarter a day. He was making more and more money himself. He still hadn't reached that day when he was "all set". Why not? He kept 'buying and investing', as he called it.

He had built a new three room shotgun type house on our property on the big road as a tenant house. This was where we had hoped he would some day build a fine home for us. He had bought and traded a new truck for a nice farm that adjoined ours. It had a nice three room house, with a barn on it. It was on the big road, too. This was to be another tenant house.

He was buying timber on the stump, which was pre-sold to different counties. He would pay so much per thousand on the stumps, so much more to have it sawn, so much to have it delivered. He was making at the rate of ten dollars per load, without even touching it; and that was real money. He figured the lumber business was better than the chicken business, and Daddy's pencil figured pretty good.

The last piece of adjoining land he had bought for the timber on it, tickled R.W.'s fancy. Daddy, not needing the land once the timber was cut, made him a real good deal on it. (Agreeing which timber he would cut, and a special type of tree he would leave.) The method with which R.W. was to pay for it, was by Daddy withholding it from his pay. (Yes, after losing Everett, I guess Daddy real-

Then There Were Two

ized a boy needed a wage.) R.W. was now nineteen years old. Of cause, he worked at making a crop for board and clothes, but in the woods in winter he got a dollar per day and board.

Everything was going great for a while. Then one day R.W. came home upset, saying that Daddy was cutting his timber. Of course, Daddy said he wasn't. The end of the dispute was R.W. gone, too. Elda and I were beside ourselves. This was too much. Our last brother gone. Now it was just her and me left, and mother was visibly shaken to the bone.

It was tension farm around there. We took R.W.'s part. For the first time in our lives, we were venting our feelings to Daddy. He took it for a while, then he informed us that he had heard enough. So, we quieted down, maybe too quiet. Poor Mama was caught in the middle. We were sullen and bitter.

R.W., doing the best thing he knew to do, joined the CCC's. Soon, he was in California. Never had one of us children been that far from home before, and Mama practically cried herself sick. Daddy, I know, felt bad too, but he was just not the kind to admit it.

Daddy still made a crop, but he tended far less acreage. Help was hard to come by in the summer, since everyone else were busy with their own crops. So Daddy plowed, and we noticed he lost weight. Elda and I were able to keep up with the hoeing, and our part of the work, but we wouldn't touch a plow. Though I had always been eager to plow, I loved to plow, but not this year. We, Elda and I, found time to hoe some for our tenants and neighbors. Thus, we were able to buy

Scrap Cotton

ourselves things that we would not have gotten otherwise.

I remember so well, we having a dollar and a half on hand between us. Daddy was gone on a business trip for the day. Elda and I were in the field, hoeing cotton. Mama brought us a jug of fresh drawn water. We got to talking about how good a Coca-Cola would taste. Mama smacked her lips. That did it! Quickly, we agreed, that I'd take half our money and go to the store. It was late June and hot. I took off the two miles to Hurt and Moore's store on foot. (The mules were in the barn, and I enjoyed riding them, but Daddy hadn't given his permission.) At the store I bought six big RC's, three bars of candy, and a twenty-five-cent cake. The colas were ice cold. But the two miles home in the hot sun, they got heavy as well as warm. Yet they tasted good to us. We had a regular feast.

There were cola and cake left over, enough for another day. The problem was, where would we put them. Daddy might get mad if he found out we had done this. We wound up putting them in the fireplace in the front room behind the big flowerpot. They would stay cool there, anyway. We assured Mama this was our doing, and she had no reason to feel guilty. We had consoled ourselves, and given Mama a treat. We felt good, Elda and I.

Chapter 75
The Three Musketeers

Most every summer after school was out, Esther would let Norma Ruth, Annie Mae, and Marie (her three oldest children) come to spend the summer months with us. When they first started coming, we were amused to no end at their lack of comprehension of life on a farm. Our cows were all boys; all our chickens were roosters; and they were full of wonder that we could get milk from a cow's udder, and they couldn't.

They were expected, of course, to help out with farming chores. Annie Mae had a terrible time distinguishing between weeds and plants. Sometimes, dressing the weeds and uprooting the plants. Sometimes scraping long spaces of all vegetation. Norma Ruth seemed to get the knack of hoeing, right away. After all, she was older. Marie was too young to endeavor to hoe, so she played around the edges for the most part. All three of them could help pick and gather fruits and vegetables, though.

Norma Ruth was getting to be quite a young lady that last year. Mama and Daddy expected that she should go with Elda and me where-ever we went, though she was younger than us. She was quite attractive to the boys, we knew. Consequently, we all started dating together. She was like another sister to us; we liked that. We had a lot of good times together.

I'll never forget her first date. These three boys had come to pick us up to go to revival meeting at Concord, some six miles away. The night before, we had had no date, so we had walked to

Scrap Cotton

church. These boys had brought us home, though. This night we had arrived early, and were still sitting in the car. Remembering, I guess, how long the walk had been the night before, and wanting to break an awkward silence as well, Norma Ruth sighed and said, "I sure dread that long walk home." Everyone laughed. Then her date asked, "Do you think we are going to make you walk home?" She was embarrased, I know, but the silence had been broken.

This was the beginning of, as we called ourselves, "The Three Musketeers." We all three did some dumb, but fun, things.

One particular night, we were out on a date with these three boys we had met at another church. We came by a cemetery where a statue of a man adorned one of the graves. We asked the boys if they knew you could walk around him three times, then ask him what he was doing, and he would say 'nothing.' They were disbelieving, yet somewhat quizzical. We assured and reassured them it was true. One of the guys jumped out and endeavored to prove to us that it wasn't. Yet, obviously, curious that it might be. He made his three complete circles, then addressed the statue as instructed. We all waited in silence, until he threw up his hands in desperation. "See! He didn't say anything." "We told you! We told you!" we chanted. "We told you he would say nothing." We laughed the poor boy to shame. Oh, well. He drove us home, but for some reason they never came back. I wonder why.....

Chapter 76
Let the Good Times Roll
1941

There just wasn't a lot of things that we were allowed to do socially in our day and in our area. There was the candy pulling, where the sorghum syrup was cooked, then cooled to the point it could be handled with greased hands. The syrup was roped and pulled, then doubled and pulled again, until it became cool and brittle.

Then there were the box suppers held by our schools. The girls would prepare a supper, then place it in a box beautifully decorated with crepe paper, complete with strips of the paper being fluted and ruffled, trimming it to perfection. The boys were not supposed to know who brought which box, therefore bidding for them, hoping a lovely girl went with the box. But if a guy was sweet on a particualr girl, someone would tip him off as to which box was hers. Then the other boys made him pay dearly. Usually the boxes went for seventy or eighty cents, some a buck or a buck and a half, while some went for as much as six or seven dollars. One year, Edith's box went for five dollars. Mine went for, let's say, considerably less than that, once I was old enough to bring one.

There were, of course, the dances or 'musics', as we called them, with the expected 'carryings-on'. A bottle or two usually infiltrated the occasion. Most of the men would nip, but noone got really drunk. There were icecream suppers where whole families got together. Then there were the chicken stews, where a couple of families got together to boil a big fat hen, add a little milk, a

Scrap Cotton

pat of butter, then crumble in a big dime box of soda crackers.

There was a honky-tonk at Silver City, complete with a big Wurlitzer Jukebox. Majestically bubbling and changing colors, it was truly fascinating, to say the least. The music was deeper and richer than what we had heard before. Very 'rich-looking' girls from Atlanta were there the night we broke all the 'rules of common decency' and went. The local boys appeared hypnotized as they twirled them gracefully around the room. This, I knew, was a 'cut above', and my eyes had seen it.

There was a movie house in Cumming, now. Lots of our local young people were going on Saturday nights, but we couldn't ever get permission to go. It was just too far out of reach for us to pretend we were going some place else, then go to the movie. The only movies I ever saw were the ones I saw at the "Traveling Cox Picture Shows" that came through each fall. They stayed for about a three night stand, showing a different picture each night. Some were silent movies, and somewhat old and flickery. One time Daddy took a basket of our Yate apples and traded them to Mr. Cox for our family to see the show. Daddy and Mama never went back, but each fall us kids could go once, at a nickle each, I believe.

The grand-daddy of all social events had to be the June singing, held in the Forsyth county courthouse. Good Gospel singers, from everywhere it seemed, were there, their music and voices being blasted from speakers on all sides of the courthouse. Take a lunch, bring a nickle or two for a coke and maybe an icecream,

Let the Good Times Roll

and spend the day in the gala atmosphere. That was living.

Only the county fair in October could top this. This fall, Elda, Norma Ruth and I took in that fair for real. We had saved two or three dollars each, and we went to give it all a whirl. Nothing was more than a nickle or a dime, and the rides really excited us. We rode them all before we were joined by these boys we knew. (Wasn't that the purpose all along?) Once the boys joined us, they wanted us to ride with them. We rode the ferris wheel, another ride or two, then on to the swings. The swings were the most challenging ride of them all. Once strapped in, they began to turn faster and faster, until everyone was flying almost straight out, around and around. The gravity pressed you into position, and it was hard to defy it.

Then there were the cigarettes we had bought before coming. I chose Chesterfields; Elda bought Lucky's; and I believe Norma Ruth bought Phillip Morris. We had been very dignified-looking, and very impressive, we were sure. We had another smoke with the boys on our way to the docile Merry-Go-Round. (That's all that was left to ride.) Elda, always being less flamboyant than me, chose for her and her boyfriend to sit in one of the carriages behind a horse. The rest of us rode astride our horses. Then on about the third or fourth round, it happened. Elda regurgitated in her lap, and on the shoes and pants' leg of her escort. When the carousel stopped, three totally embarrased girls excused ourselves, looked up the couple we had ridden with, good and ready to go home now.

Scrap Cotton

We hadn't been found out when we paid the visit to the honky-tonk, Thank God. But we had been seen at the fair smoking our cigarettes, acting a lot silly, and having a real good time. Elda being sick had been observed, as well. By whom, we never knew, but the word got back to us that we were drunk. The Lord is merciful, so it never got back to our parents. Yet, our names were mud; we just knew it. But there was not one word of truth in the drunken rumor. Why, oh, why did our one really good time have to end this way?

Chapter 77
At War

Come the fall of '41, it was Elda's time to go to Griffin. So, it had been conveniently arranged that Norma Ruth would stay with us and go to school. That way, I wouldn't be left home alone. With want of anything better to do, I went back to school part-time with her. Since our school only went to the seventh grade, I simply repeated the seventh grade.

I could have gotten a high school education, and was urged by Daddy and Mama to do so. There were school buses now, but not for me. I just didn't have the proper attire. I had, in the past, been snickered at in grammar school about my long-sleeve dresses, (homemade of course), and my ribbed stockings instead of anklets like the other girls wore. There were a lot of places that I couldn't measure up, and other kids laughed and chided. This was cruel, but children are not always diplomatic. I refused to further expose myself to this ridicule.

When Everett had left home, he soon brought us a bike. When Edith had left home, she returned in the spring with pretty clothes. Now with Elda gone, I knew she would not forget me; and she didn't. She had been gone only two weeks when the mailman brought a package from Sears & Roebuck. The excitement was overwhelming. Norma Ruth and I tore into it as fast as we could. Out came two red blazers, two navy skirts, and two white blouses. One for me, and one for Norma Ruth. They were nice, really nice, wool suits. Red, white, and blue! Patriotic colors.

Scrap Cotton

People were conciously patriotic now. I first wondered how in the world Elda had afforded my outfit on three dollars a week but learned later, that Esther had advanced her wages. This ole 'sis' had a heart to feel with. She knew the score.

The war was getting really heated up in Europe. When the Atlantic charter had been drawn up, fifteen 'axis' nations had signed it, including Russia. Yet in June, Hitler had invaded Russia, their pact in shambles. Roosevelt had changed his orders for our fleets (from 'Search and Patrol' to 'Search and Destroy'), after a Nazi ship fired on a US Destroyer. We suffered our first casualty, October 17. Two wounded, eleven missing and presumed dead. The US and the Nazis were in an undeclared war.

Germany had, up to now, proceeded cautiously toward the US, apparently fearing to antagonize us as yet. But, two weeks later, one of our escort ships was sunk carrying over a hundred of our blue-jackets to their death. The war fever was now sweeping the country. Japan, as yet, had shown no hostility toward us. Therefore, our eyes were on the Germans. By way of radio, we knew the Japanese were in Washington at this time, in an attempt to negotiate peace with us.

It was December 7, 1941, a long Sunday for Norma Ruth and I. Feeling sorry for us, I guess, Daddy let us listen to 'Grand Central Station' after the news went off. The program was interrupted. The Japs had attacked Pearl Harbor! Our entire Pacific fleet was sunk, sinking, or ablaze. The announcer was understandably shaken and distraught. I froze. (And I'm sure most of our nation experienced something similar to what I had experienced.) Shock. Horror. Dis-

At War

belief. (It was the same as with death of a loved one, that you've been expecting to expire. Though you have been looking for it, you are invaribly enveloped in shock and disbelief.) To add to the impact, war had been expected, but not from this source. Not from the Japanese.

Within three days, the world was at war, the U.S. at war with both sides of the world. The most traumatic time in our age was launched. The world, as we had known it, would be forever changed. We were fused with our allies, as brother with brother. Our enemies, though united, could not stand for long against us. We were united to the death, or until ultimate victory. We were traumatized. But God, our help in ages past, was still our help. With Him still on the throne of our nation, we would triumph again.

Once we had absorbed the shock, we were angry, determined, and confident. We would now get on with the job at hand.

Chapter 78
A New Sister-in-Law

When R.W. came back from the CCC's, he still felt hurt and resentment toward Daddy. Therefore, he got himself a boarding place with Everett and Lorene. He found himself a job at a sawmill.

It wasn't long before he became interested in fifteen year old Evelyn Kirby. She was a very pretty girl and sweet as could be. But we didn't really meet her until R.W. brought her home in late August to introduce her as his wife. She was almost sixteen by this time.

R.W. had saved most of his thirty dollars per month during the year he was in the Three C's, as well as some of the money he was making at the sawmill. But he still didn't have enough to buy a mule and set up housekeeping yet. He would try and save enough during the winter to do so, but for now they stayed with Edith and Leon.

I know Mama had hopes that Daddy and R.W. could reconcile their differences and that the newlyweds would come and live with them. The rest of us hoped so too, but both Daddy and R.W. were pretty head strong. If R.W. didn't get settled in somewhere farming, he would be drafted soon. We just didn't know how Mama would cope with that. She had taken it so hard when he was in California in the Three C's, him being so far away. But she declared she was no better than other mothers that were having to give up their sons to foreign fields.

One thing we believed for sure, Evelyn would be welcomed into the house. Mama liked her from

A New Sister-in-Law

the start. The rest of us did, too. It was nice having a new sister-in-law.

Evelyn & R.W. (Later in Life)

Chapter 79
Harvest Time
1942

With the world at war and the Japs swallowing up one island after the other in the Pacific, everyone was getting restless. Those sloppy, and somewhat ridiculous-looking, Japanese soldiers were proving their excellence in the jungle, or on the battlefield, where-ever. Therefore, no effort was spared to outfight and outmaneuver them. Everyone was pitching in or wanting to. Though we were told we were contributing to the effort by farming, somehow it just didn't seem enough. It was as if the whole country was performing methodically, while we could only stand by and gaze.

Then one day in August, with no hope of breaking that invisible barrier that stood between us and the real world. It was just before the war began to be turned around in the Pacific, when Elda and I were rendered speechless. (Elda had come home in the spring to help make a crop, as was the norm.) Mama said, "Girls, I want you to get this crop in as early as possible. Then I want you to go to Griffin, and get yourselves jobs." We stammerred and stutterred something about not leaving her alone. It would be too much on her, not having any help. She said, "No. I want you to go. There's no life for you here. I've raised you right, and I believe you will do right. You deserve better than you are getting. I'll be alright. Maybe Daddy and me will live more peacably, and enjoy ourselves more just him and me," she chided. I felt something turn over inside

Harvest Time

of me. Maybe it was my heart, I don't know. But hope had come alive within.

We had always worked hard, but this year we out-did ourselves again. We had to get us some money together to buy work clothes when we got there. We did our work. Picked our peas, and our cotton. (Daddy took care of the corn.) Then we worked for our neighbors, but we didn't get a dollar or a dollar twenty-five per day as the menfolk were now getting. We got seventy-five cents per day, or fifty cents per hundred for picking cotton. The money counted up slowly.

After the cotton crops were picked, we had but one other source to make more money: Pick our scrap cotton. And scrap cotton was just that, slim pickings. It didn't bring much money either, because the staple or grade was not that good. It was hard waiting for all the stragglely bolls to open, but we always picked our scrap cotton. A lot of people left it hang in the fields. Some obviously didn't consider it worth the effort, not needing the money that bad. Others, who we knew needed the money, just weren't that ambitious. Anyway, it made my fingers itch, seeing it go to waste in the field. Those half open bolls were rough on the cuticles, but Elda and I picked every stragglely lock we could find. Daddy hadn't planted nearly as much cotton since R.W. was gone, but we still managed to get a litte better than a hundred pounds of the knotty stuff.

Now, all that was left to do was to get it to Rosco Grogan's at Matt, two miles away, where we sold it. Daddy and us still weren't hitting it off too well. He was stubborn, and so were we. So, we didn't ask him to carry it in for us. Instead, we

Scrap Cotton

threw it over our backs and made the hike, bringing home three dollars amd sixty cents more.

Our hoard was complete. We had enough for our tickets, and thirty- two dollars each to take with us. We had planned to walk to catch our bus, but we managed to find us a ride. We had already walked to Cumming, ten miles away, to order our Social Security Cards and Birth Certificates. Now, it was only six miles to Silver City, and the Greyhound bus.

Chapter 80
A Woman's Work Is Never Done

As the bus was coming into Atlanta, being pretty well loaded by now, my thoughts turned to Mama again. Lord, I hated to be leaving her behind. She would have a lot more chores to do. The milking of the cows would surely be her job now. I just couldn't imagine Daddy milking; that had always been woman's work. We girls had been doing it for years, since it gave Mama chest pains to milk. She'd be bringing in the stove wood now, and perhaps cutting it as well. The cutting and carrying in of the firewood was mostly the men folks' job. But since R.W. had left, Elda and I did most of that. No doubt Mama would be doing a lot of that, too.

I sighed and shook my head. Elda picked up on it, and inquired if anything was wrong. "Nothing," I reassured her. My thoughts were spoiling my trip, but I couldn't shake them. Guilt was gnawing at my insides. How soon this could happen, after it was too late to correct it.

I was remembering Mama's daily routine. In the winter, it was her that got up and built the fires, cooked the breakfast, then called us to get up and eat. And if Daddy hadn't slept well, or was a little puny, she'd go feed the mules while the stove was heating. When breakfast was over, she immediately washed the dishes and slopped the hogs. (Elda made our beds while I went to milk the cows.)

Field time came with the warmer months. Mama would be through in the kitchen and ready to go to the field with the rest of us. Around 10:30

Scrap Cotton

she would head for the house, where she would make the dinner. About a quarter to twelve we would hear the old 'dinner bell,' which was just an old brake drum hung by a wire and hit with a chisel. We could hear it even in our lower bottoms.

Once dinner was over Mama would clear the table, and again wash the dishes. Daddy usually took a nap on our old homemade bunk, that sat against the wall near the fireplace in the kitchen. Depending on how long Daddy napped, was how long we got for dinner, usually until 1:00 or 1:30. After slopping the hogs, maybe Mama got to sit on the back porch and cool while she rested a few minutes.

Elda and I usually got up from the table and went to lie on the front porch, or to swing. Or if it was time for the birds to be nesting, Elda would head for the woods to look for their nests. Elda loved birds and knew every species around. She knew just about what time the little ones would be hatching. She would often put them back in their nest when they fell out. Sometimes I would go along, but I would rather hunt for guinea nests, or for a nest of a renegade hen that had 'stolen' her nest out someplace.

A tap or two on the dinner bell meant "work time" again. Mama would have her bonnet on and ready to go back to the field along with the rest of us.

In the evening, Mama would leave early again to cook afresh our supper. Elda and I again took care of feeding and milking the cows and getting in the stovewood, while Daddy fed the rest of the livestock and chickens. After supper, the same

A Woman's Work Is Never Done

routine for Mama - the dishes to wash, and the hogs to slop.

Then it was foot washing time. One foot tub for us all. We would wash as far up as we could roll our britches. Elda and I could go right to bed, if we so desired, or we could stay up and listen to Daddy talk for an hour or so. Mama would keep nodding off, and if Daddy caught her, it annoyed him. With a routine like Mama's, and the drone of Daddy's monotone voice, it was no wonder she had trouble keeping awake.

What was troubling me more right now, was why had Elda and I assumed we were more tired than Mama? Leaving her to do the dishes while we took our rest, which she undoubtedly needed worse than we did.

For the first time I almost regretted we were leaving. Elda had confided in me one day that she wanted me to marry and get away from home. She said that she had decided to always stay home with Mama, but she wanted me to be free. Thinking it over, I realized something I had known all along. We were deprived, but Mama was victimized. We could get away, but she was forever stuck to the hard duties she had taken on. I didn't want to fall into the same abyss, so I wouldn't marry either. We both had resolved to stay with Mama as long as she lived. What had happened to that resolve?

Oh God! Somehow, someway, give her the sweet rest she so greatly deserves.

Chapter 81
Bus Station
1942

Coming into Atlanta was awesome and exhilirating. The wide streets, the magnificent structures, the big trolley cars, the bustle, and (the most memorable of all) the flashing neon greyhound, giving the appearance of running on the Greyhound bus station. By this I knew the last leg of our journey was not far away.

I could not help feeling overwhelmed as we walked into the station. So big! So busy! So many people! Some were sitting patiently, while others dashed about madly. The big speakers were blaring out departures and arrivals.

We made our way to the information booth. Being told we had an hour and ten minutes to wait for a bus to Griffin, we took a seat where we could see the clock. Then we waited and watched for the minutes to tick by.

The awareness of the time in which we lived came as we watched the numerious service men milling around. Some appeared to be happy and enjoying the moment, while most of them appeared somber and intent on where they were going. A lump came into my throat. I guess I was no different from most other girls. I admired and thought them to be the most handsome young men I had ever seen. To think some of them were on their way to die on foreign soil, or in the deep of the sea. No wonder so many girls lose their hearts to service men.

The clock was moving, faster in fact, than I had anticipated. Our bus hadn't been announced

Bus Station

yet, but we decided to go outside and look for one marked "Griffin". We were glad we had, for long lines were forming at bus doors before they were opened or announced. We wouldn't want to take a chance and be left, for sure.

Funny thing, no one yet had taken a second look at my guitar strung about my neck. I was beginning to understand why though, you see a lot of unusual sights traveling. Then too, people are too preoccupied to notice anyone else. Its not that they are biggety. For, in fact, some of them are quite friendly, once they slow down long enough to take note of you.

At last we saw our bus with Griffin on the marquee above the windshield. We were among the first to get on when the driver swung open the doors. We handed him our tickets, and took a seat near the front. Then we waited for the doors to close.!

Chapter 82
Hello, Tomorrow
1942

When the bus pulled out of the terminal in Atlanta on its way to Griffin, I knew that within the hour I would step out on my new frontier; into that ever illusive 'Someday', into my promised land. Opportunity was mine to embrace. I knew there would be no turning back. Neither would I have a desire to do so. Things would be better now, I would make them better.

I knew I would visit my family whenever I reasonably could. I would always love them, and would carry them things - clothes, candy, or anything that would add a little spice to their lives. I would return to visit. But to live? Perish the thought. Things had been too hard there.

I believed I'd find a fair chance. A society that I could blend into, people who would accept me for what I was, not for how I dressed. But dress, I would. I'd make up for those years I had been deprived. I would also take my mother's teaching, and use the best grammar I knew. I'd read books until my heart was content. I'd listen to the radio without restraint. I'd see movies, as many as I wanted to see.

I believed I'd find my prince charming. We'd marry, and have a couple of the best dressed kids you ever saw. They would enjoy all the better things of life. We'd have a happy home. We'd live in the city with paved streets and white sidewalks. There would be no wood stove or fireplace. The floors would be covered with linoleum, perhaps a plush rug in the parlor. We'd

Hello, Tomorrow

have springs on our beds and ready made cotton mattresses; no feather ticks to muss up if you sat on them. And, for sure, there would be an overstuffed sofa, with pretty curtains; a radio sitting on a nice table. There would be a telephone, and taxies wating to be called.
    I knew my past life was behind me, and I believed I'd find a way to make my future better. Yes, I would 'build a future, and live in it too'. What I didn't know, and would have never believed, was that I would do the hardest work of my life when I went to work in a cotton mill. But it paid a wage, a better and better wage as the war dragged on. As my skills and abilities increased, I found my workload lighter.
    I didn't know my infatuation with clothes would be so short lived. After a couple of short years, I would feel secure in myself. I would even feel a little defiant in my dress, wearing what I liked. I just wouldn't need a lot of clothes that bad. Instead I would turn my priorities toward my home, and even a car. There would be so much more than clothes, then.
    I didn't know how I would ever be able to take the money I earned and make it 'work for me', as my Daddy used to say. I didn't know this thing yet, but I'd figure out a way. I didn't know I couldn't get far away from my mother's Christian principles, which were so deeply rooted within me. I didn't know that then, but I would find it out.
    I wouldn't have a pick-sack to sit and dream on anymore. Nor would it be cotton fields that I saw. But there would be other fields, white unto harvest; and all that I harvested would be mine.

In Loving Memory

In loving memory of my mother "Arkana Padgett Turner," who inspired me to believe in God and in myself. My father, Robert N. (Bob) Turner, who taught me how to turn a dollar. And fondly remembering my brothers now deceased: Rev. Egbert E. Turner, Everett H. Turner, and Robert W. Turner.

Mama & Daddy, 1954

Egbert Turner

Above: Everett Turner. Below: R.W. Turner